PHOTOSHOP
ELEMENTS 4

NICK VANDOME

In easy steps is an imprint of Computer Step
Southfield Road · Southam
Warwickshire CV47 0FB · United Kingdom
www.ineasysteps.com

Notice of Liability
Every effort has been made to ensure that this book contains accurate and
current information. However, Computer Step and the author shall not be
liable for any loss or damage suffered by readers as a result of any information
contained herein.

Trademarks
Photoshop® is a registered trademark of Adobe Systems Incorporated.
All other trademarks are acknowledged as belonging to their respective
companies.

Printed and bound in the United Kingdom

ISBN-13 978-1-84078-311-7
ISBN-10 1-84078-311-7

Table of Contents

Selecting areas

Layers

Text and drawing objects

Effects and filters 145

Sharing and creating 153

Printing images 175

Index 187

Introducing Photoshop Elements

Photoshop Elements 4 is an image editing program that spans the gap between very basic programs and professional-level ones. This chapter introduces the various parts of Elements 4 and shows how to quickly get up and running with this powerful and flexible program.

Covers

Chapter One

Digital imaging overview

Digital photography and image editing have rapidly become transformed from an expensive hobby for the few to a mass market business that is readily available to anyone. The standard and range of digital cameras have improved dramatically in recent years and with the emergence of software such as Photoshop Elements the exciting world of digital imaging is now within everyone's reach. When dealing with digital images there is a reasonable amount of terminology to consider.

Images with a higher number of pixels produce larger file sizes.

Pixels

These are tiny colored dots that are the building blocks of digital images. The word comes from a contraction of "picture element" and every image captured with a digital camera or a scanner will contain thousands of pixels. The more pixels there are in an image, generally, the better as far as the quality is concerned. This is particularly true if the image is going to be printed. The size of an image is usually described in terms of its height and width in pixels, or as these dimensions multiplied together.

Resolution

This is a term that is used to describe a number of things in the world of digital imaging:

The print resolution of an image is also known as the document size, which refers to the size at which it will be printed.

- Image resolution. This is the physical size of an image, measured in pixels

- Monitor resolution. This is the number of pixels that can be displayed in a linear inch on a computer monitor (usually 72–96 pixels per inch)

- Print resolution. This affects the size at which an image can be printed. The print resolution can be altered in the image editing software to alter the print size. A higher print resolution gives a better quality but a smaller image than one with a lower resolution

Image editing software

These are the programs that enhance and improve the basic image from a digital camera or a scanner. The world of image editing is an exciting and versatile one and Photoshop Elements is setting new standards in this field.

Through the use of a program such as Elements, digital images can be improved and altered dramatically:

Original

HOT TIP

Special effects can be added to a whole image, or they can be added to an area that has been selected within an image. For more information on selecting areas, see Chapter Six.

Improve color and lighting

Add special effects

Add shapes and text

About Elements

Photoshop Elements is the offspring of the professional-level image editing program, Photoshop. Photoshop is somewhat unusual in the world of computer software in that it is widely accepted as being the best program of its type on the market. If professional designers or photographers are using an image editing program it will almost certainly be Photoshop. However, two of the potential drawbacks to Photoshop are the cost (approximately $600) and its complexity. This is where Elements comes into its own. Adobe (the makers of Photoshop and Elements) have recognized that the majority of digital imaging users (i.e. the consumer market) want something with the basic power of Photoshop but with enough user-friendly features to make it easy to use. With the explosion in the digital camera market a product was needed to meet the needs of a new generation of image editors and that product is Elements.

Photoshop Elements 4 is only available for PCs using Windows XP. At the time of writing there is no version for the Mac.

Elements 4 contains the same powerful editing/color management tools as the full version of Photoshop and it also includes a number of versatile features for sharing images and for creating artistic projects such as slide shows, cards, calendars and photo galleries for the Web. It also has valuable help features:

Photoshop Elements can be bought for under $100 and can be purchased online from computer and software sites or at computer software stores. It is also bundled with a lot of digital cameras/scanners.

The How To palette explains what different items can be used for and gives a step-by-step guide to various digital editing techniques

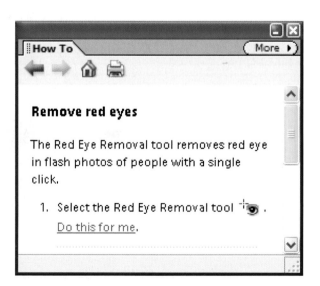

Special effects

One of the great things about using Elements with digital images is that it provides numerous fun and creative options for turning mediocre images into eye-catching works of art. This is achieved through a wide variety of filters and effects:

The histogram displays the tonal range of the colors in an image.

Advanced features

In addition to user-friendly features, Elements also has more advanced functions such as the histogram:

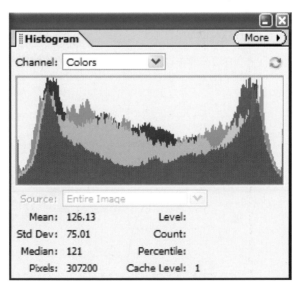

Welcome Screen

When you first open Elements you will be presented with the Welcome Screen. This offers initial advice about working with Elements and also provides options for creating new files or opening existing ones. The Welcome Screen appears by default but this can be altered once you become more familiar with Elements.

Welcome Screen functions

The Welcome Screen can be accessed at any time by selecting Window> Welcome from the Menu bar.

1. Options for organizing photos, fixing them, editing them, creating cards and calendars and creating files from scratch

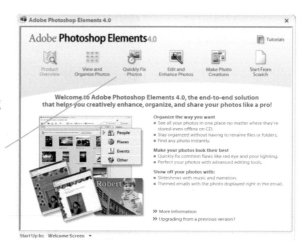

2. Roll over an item to see its details

3. Click here to select whether the Welcome Screen is displayed at start-up

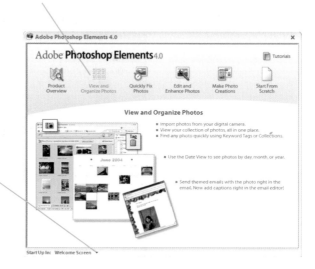

Editor mode

Once the Welcome Screen has been exited, the standard Elements interface is available. This is a combination of the work area (where images are opened and edited), menus, toolbars, a toolbox and palettes. At first it can seem a little daunting, but Elements has been designed to offer as much help as possible as you proceed through the digital editing process.

The components of the Elements interface are:

Editor mode has a Standard Edit function and a Quick Fix option. Standard Edit is used for general, and advanced, image editing while Quick Fix can be used for automated editing.

Menu bar   Shortcuts bar   Options bar   Palettes bin

Toolbox   Work area   Open palettes

Photo Bin

The Photo Bin is a feature that can be accessed from the Editor in either Standard Edit or Quick Fix mode. The Photo Bin enables you to quickly access all of the images that you have open within the Editor. To use the Photo Bin:

1 Open two or more images. The most recently opened one will be the one that is active in the Editor

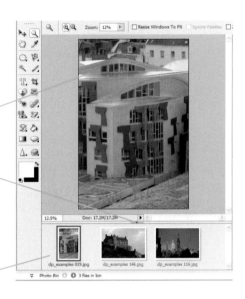

2 Click here to expand or collapse the Photo Bin

3 All open images are shown here in the Photo Bin

Images can also be made active for editing by dragging them directly from the Photo Bin and dropping them within the Editor window.

4 Click on an image in the Photo Bin to make that the active one for editing

Organizer mode

The Organizer mode contains a number of functions for sorting, viewing and finding multiple images. To use the Organizer:

1. In Editor mode, click on the Photo Browser button

2. The Photo Browser displays thumbnails of your photos and also has functions for sorting and finding images

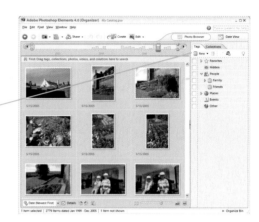

Both the Photo Browser and Date View are components of the Organizer.

3. In either the Photo Browser or the Editor, click on the Date View button

4. This displays a calendar interface that can be used to view images that were captured on a specific date. Click here to move through the calendar

Images displayed in the Photo Browser can be located anywhere on your computer. The thumbnails in Photo Browser are just references to the originals.

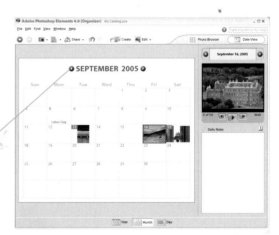

Creation mode

Creation mode is where you can release your artistic flair and start designing cards, calendars and photo albums. It can also be used to create slide shows, put your images onto disc using the VCD format and create Web photo galleries. To use Creation mode:

1   In either the Editor or the Organizer, click on the Create button

2   Click here to access one of the Creation projects. Each project has its own wizard that takes you through the process

3   Creation mode can be used to create a variety of artistic projects, containing your own images

Winter scene
Hi from the frozen north

Shortcuts bar

The Shortcuts bar provides quick access to some of the most commonly used features within Elements. The Shortcuts bar is visible at all times and is one of the most commonly used areas of Elements. Most of the options in the Shortcuts bar can be accessed from the Menu bar (generally through the File menu) but it is very useful to have the options represented as icons. Tooltip descriptions appear for each icon when you roll over them.

Editor Shortcuts bar items

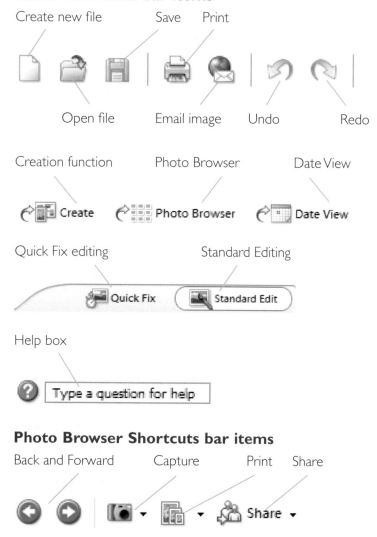

Photo Browser Shortcuts bar items

Menu bar

In the Editor, the Menu bar contains menus that provide all of the functionality for the workings of Elements. Some of these functions can also be achieved through the use of the other components of Elements, such as the Toolbox, the Shortcuts bar, the Options bar and the palettes. However, the Menu bar is where all of the commands needed for the digital editing process can be accessed in one place.

Menu bar menus

Elements does not support the CMYK color model for editing digital images. This could be an issue if you use a commercial printer.

- File. This has standard commands for opening, saving and printing images, and also commands for creating panoramas (Photomerge) and accessing online services from Adobe

- Edit. This contains commands for undoing previous operations, and standard copy and paste techniques

- Image. This contains commands for altering the size, shape and position of an image. It also contains more advanced functions such as changing the color mode of an image

- Enhance. This contains commands for editing the color elements of an image. It also contains quick-fix options

- Layer. This contains commands for working with different layers within an image

- Select. This contains commands for working with areas that have been selected within an image with one of the selection tools in the Toolbox

- Filter. This contains numerous filters that can be used to apply special effects to an image

- View. This contains commands for changing the size at which an image is displayed and also options for showing or hiding rulers and grid lines

- Window. This contains commands for changing the way multiple images are displayed and also options for displaying all of the components of Elements

- Help. This contains the various Help options

Toolbox

The Toolbox contains tools for adding items to an image (such as shapes and text), selecting areas of an image and also for applying editing techniques. Some of the tools have more than one option, in which case they have a small black triangle at the bottom right of the default tool. To access additional tools in the Toolbox:

Click and hold here to access additional tools for a particular item

The tools that have additional options are: the Marquee tools, the Lasso tools, the Magic Selection Brush tool, the Healing Brush tools, the Type tools, the Eraser tools, the Brush tools, the Stamp tools, the Object tools (e.g. the Rectangle tool), the Blur tool and the Sponge tool.

For full details of the Toolbox functions, see the Handy Reference page at the front of the book.

Working with the Toolbox

By default, the Toolbox is docked at the left of the main Editor window. However, it can be removed and dragged anywhere within the main window. To do this:

1 Click and drag here to undock the Toolbox

2 Click and drag here to move the Toolbox around the Editor window. Drag it back to its original location to redock it at the left of the window

Options bar

The Options bar provides attributes that can be set for a selected tool from the Toolbox. For instance, if the Eraser tool is selected, the Options bar offers choices for the type of eraser that can be used, its size, its mode and its opacity level. For each tool, a different set of options is available from the Options bar.

Using the Options bar

1 Click on a tool in the Toolbox (in this example it is the Magic Wand tool)

2 Select the options for the tool in the Options bar

If a tool has more than one option in the Toolbox, these are all displayed on the Options bar. Clicking on a different tool on the Options bar changes the currently selected tool in the Toolbox.

Tolerance: 32 ☑ Anti-alias ☑ Contiguous ☐ Sample All Layers

3 Apply the tool to an image. The tool will maintain the settings in the Options bar until they are changed

Palettes

Elements uses palettes to group together similar editing functions and provide quick access to certain techniques. The available palettes are:

- Info. This displays information about an image, or a selected element within it. This includes details about the color in an image or the position of a certain item

- How To. This offers advice on how to achieve particular digital imaging techniques. Each technique has a step-by-step guide and some of the steps are performed automatically by following links within the How To palette

- Layers. This enables several layers to be included within an image. This can be useful if you want to add elements to an existing image, such as shapes or text. Layers can also be used to merge two separate images together. This is one of the most powerful devices when working with digital images

- Styles and Effects. This contains special effects and styles that can be applied to an entire image or a selected part of an image. There are also filters which have their own dialog boxes in which settings can be applied and adjusted. Layer Styles can also be applied to elements within an image

- Color Swatches. This is a palette for selecting colors that can then be applied to parts of an image or elements that have been added to it

- Undo History. This can be used to undo all, or some, of the editing steps that have been performed. Every action that has been applied to an image is displayed in the Undo History palette and these actions can be reversed by dragging the slider at the side of the palette upwards

- Navigator. This can be used to move around an image and magnify certain areas of it

- Histogram. This displays a graph of the tonal range of the colors in an image. It is useful for assessing the overall exposure of an image and it changes as an image is edited

The palettes are located in the Palettes Bin which is at the right of the Editor window. This can be collapsed or expanded by clicking on the small arrow in the middle of the left-hand border of the bin.

The Undo History palette can be used to step backwards through earlier stages of the editing process.

Working with palettes

By default all palettes are minimized and grouped in the Palette Bin. However, it is possible to open one or more palettes so that they are displayed independently from the Palette Bin. To work with palettes:

1 Palettes are grouped together in the Palette Bin at the right of the work area

2 Click and drag here to move a palette away from the bin (or move a detached palette back into the bin)

Don't have too many palettes open at one time. If you do, the screen will become cluttered and it will be difficult to edit images effectively.

3 Click here to view a palette's menu

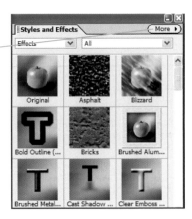

4 Every palette has its own menu; its options depend on the functions within the palette

Preferences

A number of preferences can be set within Elements to determine the way the program operates. It is perfectly acceptable to leave all of the default settings as they are, but as you become more familiar with the program you may want to change some of the preference settings. Preferences can be accessed by selecting Edit>Preferences from the Menu bar, and the available ones are:

- General. This contains a variety of options for selecting items such as shortcut keys

- Saving Files. This determines the way Elements saves files

- Display & Cursors. This determines how cursors operate when certain tools are selected

- Transparency. This determines the color, or transparency, of the background on which an open image resides

- Units & Rulers. This determines the unit of measurement used by items such as rulers

- Grid. This determines the color and format of any grid

Each preference has its own dialog box in which the specific preference settings can be made.

- Plug-Ins & Scratch Disks. This determines how Elements allocates disk space when processing editing tasks. If you require more memory for editing images (image editing can be a very memory-intensive process) you can do this by allocating up to four scratch disks on your hard drive. These act as extra areas from which memory can be used during the editing process

- Memory & Image Cache. This determines how Elements allocates memory when processing editing tasks

- Type. This determines the way text appears when it is added to images

The Organize & Share preferences can be accessed by selecting Edit> Preferences from the Menu bar in either Editor mode or Organizer mode.

- Organize & Share. These preferences open in the Organizer mode and offer a collection of preferences that are applicable to these functions. These are General, Files, Folder Location View, Editing, Camera or Card Reader, Scanner, Calendar, Tags and Collections, Mobile Phone, Sharing and Services

Getting help

One of the differences between Elements and the full version of Photoshop is the amount of assistance and guidance offered by each program. Since Photoshop is aimed more at the professional end of the market, the level of help is confined largely to the standard help directory that serves as an online manual. Elements also contains this, but in addition it has the How To palette which is designed to take users through the digital image editing process as smoothly as possible. The How To palette offers general guidance about digital imaging techniques and there are also help items that can be accessed by selecting Help from the Menu bar. These include online help, information on available plug-ins for Elements, tutorials and support details.

Using the help files

Select Photoshop Elements Help from the Help menu and click Contents or Index. Then click once on an item to display it in the main window

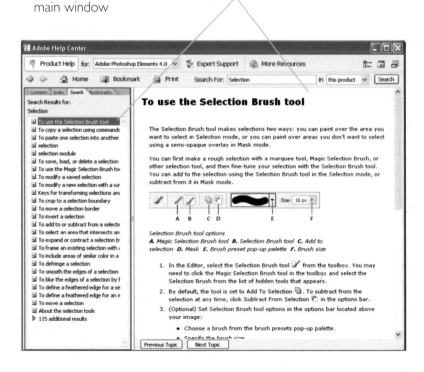

Organizing images

This chapter shows how to download digital images via Elements and then how to view and organize them. It also shows how to open, save and create image files.

Covers

Chapter Two

Obtaining images

One of the first tasks in Elements is to download images so that you can start editing and sharing them. This can be done from a variety of devices but the process is similar for all of them. To download images into Elements:

For a lot of digital cameras the Photo Downloader window will appear automatically once the camera is connected to the computer.

1 Access the Photo Browser by clicking on this button in the Editor

2 Click here and select the type of device from which you want to load images into Elements

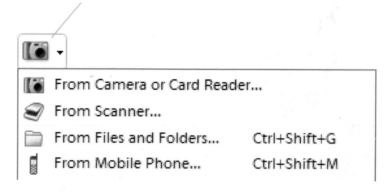

Images can also be downloaded from existing files and folders on a computer. This means that they will be added to the Photo Browser database and you will be able to apply all of its features to the images.

3 Click here to select a specific device

Elements 4 has the capability for downloading and editing RAW images and those with 16-bit color depth. These produce high quality images and are usually available on higher specification digital cameras. However, both RAW and 16-bit images are becoming more common in consumer digital cameras. When RAW images are opened in Elements the Camera Raw dialog box opens and various editing functions can be applied to the image. RAW images act as a digital negative and have to be saved into another format before they can be used in the conventional way.

4 All of the images on the selected device are displayed. Check the boxes next to images to select them for downloading

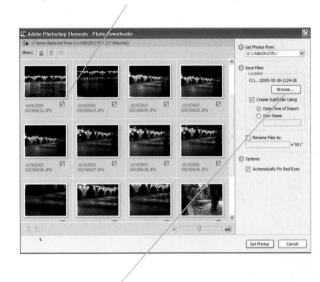

5 Click here to select a destination for the selected images and click the Get Photos button to download them

6 The downloaded images are then displayed on their own in the Photo Browser. Click here to view all of the photos that have been added within the Photo Browser

In the Organizer, select View> Arrangement> Import Batch from the Menu bar to view the images according to the date on which they were imported into the Photo Browser.

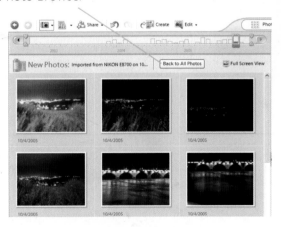

Photo Browser

The Photo Browser is the function within the Organizer that is used to view, find and sort images. When using the Photo Browser, images have to be actively added to it so it can then catalog them. Once images have been downloaded, the Photo Browser acts as a window for viewing and sorting your images no matter where they are located. Aspects of the Photo Browser include:

The Photo Browser can be set to watch specific folders on your computer. Whenever images are added to these folders, or edited within them, you will be prompted to add them into the Photo Browser. To specify folders to be watched, select File>Watch Folders from the Photo Browser Menu bar and then browse to the folder, or folders, that you want to include. This ensures that images in different locations will still be updated by the Photo Browser.

1 Timeline for viewing images that were downloaded at a certain time

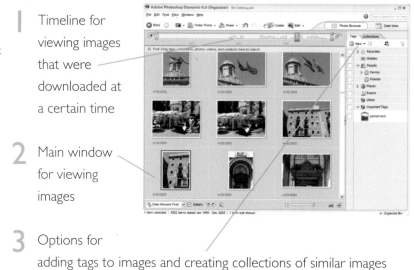

2 Main window for viewing images

3 Options for adding tags to images and creating collections of similar images

4 Toolbar for viewing images:

The toolbar for selecting how images are displayed is at the bottom of the Photo Browser window.

Date order for viewing   File details   Image Orientation

Properties

Magnification slider for changing the size at which images are viewed in the main window

Accessing images

To access images within the Photo Browser:

1 Drag this button on the Timeline to view images that were captured or downloaded on different dates

2 Drag here to scroll through images within the main window

3 Double-click on an image to view it in the whole Photo Browser window

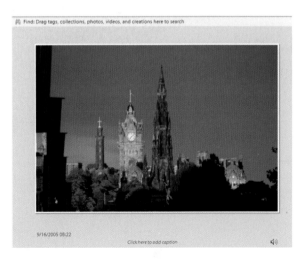

Full Screen Review

From within the Photo Browser it is possible to view all of your images, or a selection of them, at full screen size. In addition, music can be added to create an impressive slide show effect. To use the Full Screen Review:

If you do not select specific images to view in Full Screen Review, the whole Photo Browser catalog will be included. To select specific files, click on one image and then hold down Ctrl and click on subsequent ones.

1   In the Photo Browser, click this button on the toolbar, or press F11

2   Select the viewing options and click OK

3   Click here to collapse or expand the pane of available images

Press Esc to return to the Photo Browser from either Full Screen Review or Full Screen Compare.

4   Playback tools

5   Magnification tools

Full Screen Compare

In addition to viewing individual images at full screen size, it is also possible to compare two images next to each other. This can be a very useful way of checking the detail of similar images, particularly for items such as focus and lighting. To compare images using Full Screen Compare:

1 In Full Screen Review, click here on the toolbar and select an option for comparing images

2 Click on two images in the image pane

Only two images can be compared at the same time in Full Screen Compare. If you select a third image while in Full Screen Compare, this will replace one of the other two images.

3 Click on this button on the toolbar. This enables zooming on both images simultaneously

Full Screen Compare is a good way to compare two similar images as far as their image quality is concerned.

4 Drag on this slider or click the zoom icon

5 The images are displayed and the zoom command is applied to both of them

Stacks

Since digital cameras make it quick, easy and cheap to capture dozens, or hundreds, of images on a single memory card it is no surprise that most people are now capturing more images than ever before. One result of this is that it is increasingly tempting to take several shots of the same subject, just to try and capture the perfect image. The one drawback with this is that when it comes to organizing your images on a computer it can become time-consuming to work your way through all of your near-identical shots. The Photo Browser offers a useful solution to this by enabling the stacking of similar images so that you can view a single thumbnail rather than several. To do this:

You can remove images from a stack by selecting the stack in the Photo Browser and selecting Edit>Stack>Flatten Stack from the Menu bar. However, this will remove all of the images, apart from the top one, from the Photo Browser. This does not remove them from your hard drive, although there is an option to do this if you wish.

1 Select the images that you want to stack in the Photo Browser

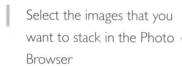

2 Select Edit>Stack>Stack Selected Photos from the Menu bar

3 The images are stacked into a single thumbnail and the existence of the stack is indicated by this icon

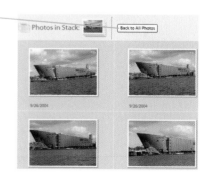

To revert stacked images to their original state, select Edit> Stack>Unstack Photos from the Menu bar.

4 To view all of the stacked images, select Edit>Stack>Reveal Photos in Stack from the Menu bar

5 Click here to return to all of the photos in the Photo Browser

Version sets

When working with digital images it is commonplace to create several different versions from a single image. This could be to use one for printing and one for use on the Web or because there are elements of an image that you want to edit. Instead of losing track of images that have been edited it is possible to create stacked thumbnails of edited images, which are known as version sets. These can include the original image and all of the edited versions. Version sets can be created and added to from either the Photo Browser or the Editor. To do this:

1 In the Photo Browser, select an image

2 Make editing changes to the image in either standard edit or Quick Fix mode

3 Select Edit>Save As from the Menu bar

4 Check on the Save in Version Set with Original box and click Save

5 A dialog box alerts you to the fact that the image has been edited but the original has not been altered. Click OK

6 The original image and the edited one are grouped together in a stack and the fact that it is a version set is denoted by this icon

The other version set menu options are Flatten Version Set, and Revert to Original. The latter deletes all of the other versions except the original.

7 To view all of the images in a version set, select the set and select File>Version Set>Reveal Photos in Version Set from the Menu bar

Tagging images

As your digital image collection begins to grow on your computer it is increasingly important to be able to keep track of your images and find the ones you want, when you want them. One way of doing this is by assigning specific tags to images. You can then search for images according to the tags that have been added to them. The tagging function is accessed from the Organize Bin within the Organizer. To add tags to images:

The Organize Bin can also be accessed by selecting Window> Organize Bin from the Photo Browser Menu bar.

1 If the Organize Bin is not visible, click here at the bottom right of the Photo Browser or click here on the right border of the Photo Browser to expand the Organize Bin

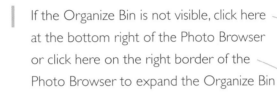

2 Click here to access the currently available tags

When you create a new category you can choose a new icon for the category too.

3 Click here to access sub-categories for a particular category

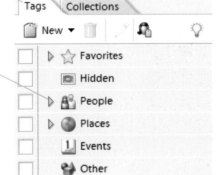

4 Click here to add categories or sub-categories of your own choice

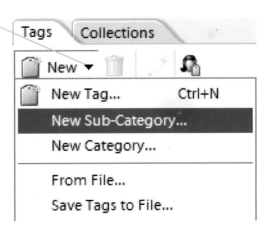

5 Enter a name for the new category or sub-category and click OK

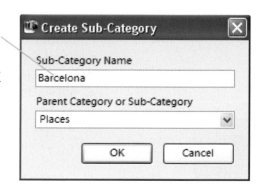

6 Select the required images in the Photo Browser

7 Drag a tag onto one of the selected images

8 The images are tagged with the icon that denotes the main category, rather than the sub-category

Tagging faces

Most people with digital cameras capture a lot of images of people, usually family and friends. It is possible to tag these images in the same way as any others and Elements makes the process as straightforward as possible with the Face Tagging function. This works by Elements looking through all of the images in the Organizer and automatically identifying the ones that contain faces. These are displayed and tags can then be applied to match names with faces. To do this:

If Elements looks through your whole catalog for images containing faces it can take a long time, depending on the number of images that are stored.

1 In the Organizer, select Find>Find Faces for Tagging from the Menu bar

2 All images with faces are displayed in the Face Tagging window

Faces for tagging can also be accessed by selecting specific images first and then selecting Find>Find Faces for Tagging from the Menu bar. This makes the process quicker but it could result in you missing some images with the relevant faces in them.

3 Click here and select a New Category or a New Sub-Category

4 Enter a name for the Sub-Category and/or Category

5 Click OK

6 Select specific images by clicking on them or dragging around them with the cursor

The process of finding faces in images is not foolproof. If you want to exclude some of the resultant images from the face tagging process, select them in the Face Tagging window and click on the Don't Tag Selected Item(s) button at the top right of the window.

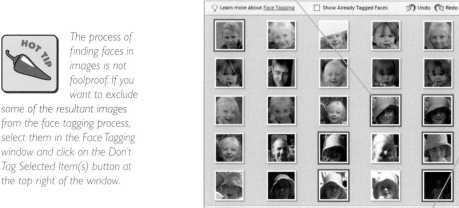

7 Drag a tag onto one of the selected images. The tag is applied to all of the selected images

8 Click here to display all of the tagged images

Tagged faces can also have other tags attached to them. This enables a more refined search process when looking for people in certain situations or at certain periods of time.

9 The images are displayed in full, rather than just the faces as in the Face Tagging window

Creating collections

Another way of organizing images for sorting and searching is to group them into collections. To do this:

1 Click here in the Organize Bin to access the collections

2 Click here to create a new collection

3 Click here to browse for an icon to denote the collection

4 Enter a name for the collection here

5 Add any notes about the collection

6 Click OK

7 The new collection is added under the Collections tab

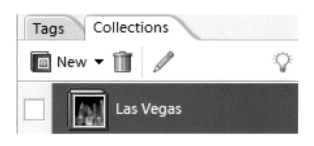

8 Select the required images in the Photo Browser and drag the collection's icon onto one of the selected images

Collections can be viewed in Full Screen Review in the same way as viewing separate images within the Photo Browser.

9 The images are tagged with the collection's icon

Searching for images

Once images have been tagged, or sorted into collections, they can be searched for using both of these options. To do this:

1 For tags and collections, click on this box so that the binoculars are showing

If more than one set of tags or collections are specified for a search as shown in Step 1, all of the matching images will be displayed, not just those for a single search.

2 For tags and collections, drag one of the icons here below the timeline in the Photo Browser

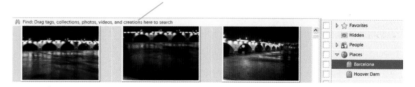

3 All matching items for a search are shown together within the Photo Browser. Click here to return to the rest of the images

You can also search for items by using the Find command on the Menu bar. This can be used to search for images, video clips, audio clips and creations.

Searching by metadata

Metadata for digital images is information about the images themselves. It can be created by a lot of digital cameras when the images are captured. For instance, a camera may record the camera model, the date of capture, the size (in pixels) and a variety of image information such as shutter speed and exposure settings. This information is retained when images are downloaded by Elements and it can then be used to search for images with specific attributes. To do this:

1 Access the Organizer and select Find>By Details (Metadata) from the Menu bar

Searching by metadata is an excellent way to find images captured under certain shooting conditions, as the information is taken directly from the details stored by the camera.

2 Click here to access the available metadata fields

3 Click here to add search criteria

4 Click Search to find images that match the metadata criteria

5 The matching images are displayed in the Photo Browser and the search criteria are noted here

Date View

Date View is a function that offers the facility for viewing downloaded images in a calendar format. This can be viewed for either a year, a month or a day. The images are placed in the calendar according to the date on which they were captured, edited or downloaded. To use Date View:

1 In either the Editor or the Photo Browser, click on this button

2 Click here to move through the calendar

3 Double-click on an image to view all of the items for that specific day in the full window

Click on the name of a month at the top of a calendar to see a list of available years. Those with an icon next to them contain photos.

⦿ SEPTEMBER 2005 ⦿

Sun	Mon	Tue	Wed	Thu	Fri	Sat
				1	2	3
4	5	6	7	8	9	10
11	12 Labor Day	13	14	15	16	17
18	19	20	21	22	23	24
25	26	27	28	29	30	

4 Select a day and click here to view all of the images for that day in a slide show

September 16, 2005

21 of 182   06:48

5 Select an option here to view the calendar in Year, Month or Day format

Year   Month   Day

Opening images

Once you have captured images with a digital camera or a scanner and stored them on your computer you can then open them in Elements. There are a number of options for this:

Open command

1 Select File>Open from the Menu bar or click the Open button in the Shortcuts bar:

2 Select an image from your hard drive and click Open

Another option for opening files is the Open Recently Edited File command, which is accessed from the File menu. This lists the files you have opened most recently.

Open As command

This can be used to open a file in a different file format from its original format. To do this:

1 Select File>Open As from the Menu bar

2 Select an image and select the file format here. Click Open

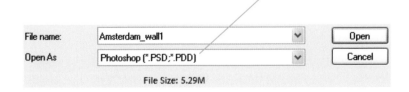

Creating new files

On some occasions it is useful to be able to open a new, blank file. This could be if you want to combine two or more images and you are not sure of the final size of the image, or if you have copied part of an image and you want to paste it into a new file. New files can also be useful for creating images from scratch. To create a new, blank file:

1 Select File>New Blank File from the Menu bar or click on the New button on the Shortcuts bar

2 Enter the dimensions of the file and also its resolution, which will affect the size when printed

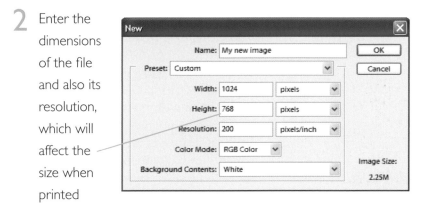

A resolution setting of 200 or above will ensure a high-quality printed image.

3 Click OK

4 The new, blank file is created and content can now be added to it

Saving images

File formats

When saving digital images, it is always a good idea to save them in at least two different file formats, particularly if layered elements such as text and shapes have been added. One of these formats should be the proprietary Photoshop format PSD or PDD. The reason for using this is that it will retain all of the layered information within an image. So if a text layer has been added, this will still be available for editing at a future date, once it has been saved and closed.

A proprietary file format is one that is specific to the program being used. It has greater flexibility when used within the program itself but cannot be distributed as easily as a JPEG or a GIF image can.

The other format that an image should be saved in is the one most appropriate for the use to which it is going to be put. Therefore, images that are going to be used on the Web should be saved as JPEG, GIF or PNG files, while an image that is going to be used for printing should be saved in a format such as TIFF. Once images have been saved in these formats, all of the layered information within them becomes flattened into a single layer and it will not be possible to edit this once the image has been saved. By default, images are saved in the same format as the one in which they were opened. Most image formats have dialog boxes for options when they are being saved, like this one for JPEGs:

The Save As command should be used if you want to make a copy of an image with a different file name. Editing changes can then be made to the copy, while the original remains untouched.

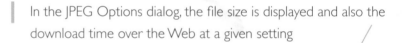

In the JPEG Options dialog, the file size is displayed and also the download time over the Web at a given setting

By default, the Save As command saves an image in the same format as the one in which it was opened.

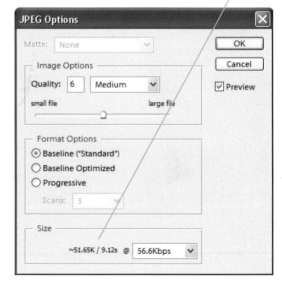

First digital steps

This chapter shows how to get up and running with digital image editing and details some effective editing techniques for improving digital images.

Covers

Chapter Three

Color enhancements

Some of the simplest but most effective editing changes that can be made to digital images are color enhancements. These can help to transform a mundane image into a stunning one and Elements offers a variety of methods for achieving this. Some of these are verging towards the professional end of image editing while others are done almost automatically by Elements. These are known as Auto adjustments and some simple manual adjustments can also be made to the brightness and contrast of an image. All of these color enhancement features can be accessed from the Enhance menu on the Menu bar.

Auto Levels

This automatically adjusts the overall color tone in an image in relation to the lightest and darkest points in the image:

Another Auto command on the Enhance menu is Auto Smart Fix. This can be used to automatically edit all of the color balance of an image in one step. However, the results can sometimes be less than perfect so it is important to review the changes carefully to make sure they are better than the original.

Auto Contrast

This automatically adjusts the contrast in an image:

If you do not like the color enhancement once it has been applied to the image, click on the Step Backward button on the Shortcuts bar.

Auto Color Correction

This automatically adjusts all the color elements within an image:

Apply small amounts of Brightness and Contrast at a time when you are editing an image. This will help ensure that the end result does not look too unnatural.

Adjust Brightness/Contrast

This can be used to manually adjust the brightness and contrast in an image:

1   Select Enhance>Adjust Lighting>Brightness/Contrast from the Menu bar

2   Drag these sliders to adjust the image brightness and contrast

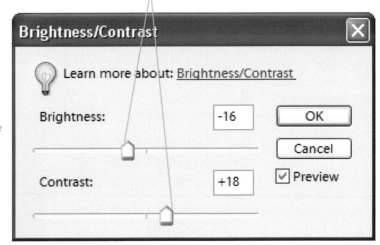

Always make sure that the Preview box is checked when you are applying color enhancements. This will display the changes as you make them and before they are applied to the image.

3   Click OK

Adjust Shadows/Highlights

One problem that most photographers encounter at some point is where part of an image is exposed correctly while another part is either over- or under-exposed. If this is corrected using general color correction techniques such as levels or brightness and contrast, the poorly exposed area may be improved, but at the expense of the area that was correctly exposed initially. To overcome this the Shadows/Highlights command can be used to adjust particular tonal areas of an image. To do this:

1 Open an image where one part is correctly exposed and another part is incorrectly exposed

Adjusting shadows can make a significant improvement to an image in which one area is underexposed and the rest is correctly exposed.

2 Select Enhance>Adjust Lighting>Shadows/Highlights from the Menu bar

3 Make the required adjustments using the sliders or by entering figures in the boxes

4 Click OK

5 The poorly exposed areas of the image have been corrected, without altering the rest of the properly exposed image

Cropping

Cropping is a technique that can be used to remove unwanted areas of an image and highlight the main subject. The area to be cropped can only be selected as a rectangle. To crop an image:

1 Select the Crop tool from the Toolbox:

2 Click and drag on an image to select the area to be cropped. The area that is selected is retained and the area to be cropped appears grayed-out

The Options bar for the Crop tool has an option for selecting preset sizes for the crop tool. This results in the crop being in specific proportions. For instance, if you want to print an image at 10 x 8 size, you can use this preset crop size to ensure that the cropped image is at the correct proportions for this. The image dialog box will also be updated accordingly.

3 Click and drag here to resize the crop area

4 Click on the check mark to accept the changes and the circle to reject them

Cloning

Cloning is a technique that can be used to copy one area of an image over another. This can be used to cover up small imperfections in an image, such as a dust mark or a spot, and also to copy or remove large items in an image such as a person.

To clone items:

1 Select the Clone Stamp tool from the Toolbox:

2 Set the Clone Stamp options in the Options bar

3 Hold down Alt and click on the image to select a source point from which the cloning will start

DSCN2632.JPG @ 25% (RGB/8)

4 Drag the cursor to copy everything over which the selection point marker passes

Pattern cloning

The Pattern Stamp tool can be used to copy a selected pattern over an image, or a selected area of an image. To do this:

The Pattern Stamp tool is grouped in the Toolbox with the Clone Stamp tool. It can be selected from the Options bar or by clicking and holding on the black triangle in the corner of the Clone Stamp tool and then selecting the Pattern Stamp tool from the subsequent list.

1 Select the Pattern Stamp tool from the Toolbox:

2 Click here in the Options bar to select a pattern

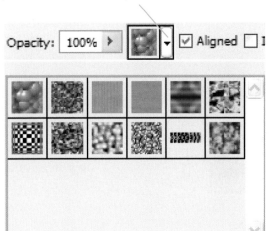

Patterns can be added to the patterns palette by selecting an image, or an area of an image, and selecting Edit> Define Pattern from the Menu bar. Then give the pattern a name in the Pattern Name dialog box and click OK.

3 Click and drag on an image to copy the selected pattern over it

Healing Brush

One of the favorite techniques in digital imaging is removing unwanted items, particularly physical blemishes such as spots and wrinkles. This can be done with the Clone tool but the effects can sometimes be too harsh as a single area is copied over the affected item. A more subtle effect can be achieved with the Healing Brush and the Spot Healing Brush tools. The Healing Brush can be used to remove blemishes over larger areas, such as wrinkles:

1 Open an image with blemishes covering a reasonably large area i.e. more than a single spot

The Healing Brush tool is more subtle than the Clone tool as it blends the copied area together with the area over which it is copying. This is particularly effective on people as it preserves the overall skin tone better than the Clone tool does.

2 Select the Healing Brush tool from the Toolbox and make the required selections in the Options bar

3 Hold down Alt and click on an area of the image to load the Healing Brush tool. Drag over the affected area. The cross is the area which is copied beneath the circle. At this point the overall tone is not perfect and looks too pink

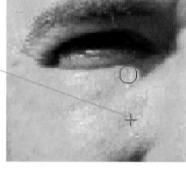

4 Release the mouse and the Healing Brush blends the affected area with the one that was copied over it. This creates a much more natural skin tone

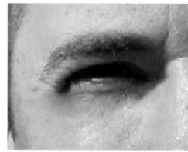

Spot Healing Brush

The Spot Healing Brush is very effective for quickly removing small blemishes in an image, such as spots. To do this:

1 Open an image and zoom in on the area with the blemish

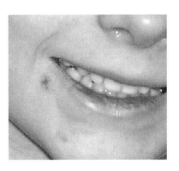

2 Select the Spot Healing Brush tool from the Toolbox and make the required selections in the Options bar

When dragging over a blemish with the Spot Healing Brush tool, make sure the brush size is larger than the area of the blemish. This will ensure that you can cover the blemish in a single stroke.

3 Drag the Spot Healing Brush tool over the affected area

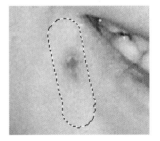

4 The blemish is removed and the overall skin tone is retained

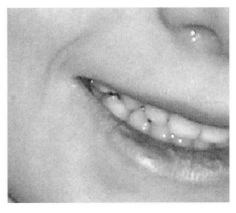

Rotating

Various rotation commands can be applied to images and also individual layers in layered images. This can be useful for positioning items and also for correcting the orientation of an image that is on its side or upside down.

Rotating a whole image

1 Select Image>Rotate from the Menu bar

2 Select a rotation option from the menu

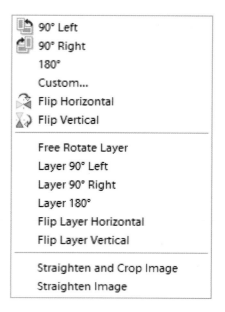

90° Left
90° Right
180°
Custom...
Flip Horizontal
Flip Vertical

Free Rotate Layer
Layer 90° Left
Layer 90° Right
Layer 180°
Flip Layer Horizontal
Flip Layer Vertical

Straighten and Crop Image
Straighten Image

3 Select Custom to enter your own value for the amount you want an image rotated

If an image is only slightly misaligned, then only a small angle figure is required in the Rotate Canvas dialog box. A figure of 1 or 2 can sometimes be sufficient.

Rotate Canvas

Angle: 5   ⊙ °Right   OK
              ○ °Left   Cancel

4 Click OK

Rotating a layer

If an image is made up of two or more layers, these can be rotated independently from one another. To rotate a layer:

1 Open an image that consists of two or more layers. Select one of the layers

For more information about working with layers, see Chapter Seven.

2 Select Image> Rotate from the Menu bar

By default, images are opened with no regular layers, just the background layer, which is locked.

3 Select a layer rotation option from the menu

Free Rotate Layer
Layer 90° Left
Layer 90° Right
Layer 180°
Flip Layer Horizontal
Flip Layer Vertical

4 The selected layer is rotated independently from the rest of the image

Transforming

The Transform commands can be used to resize an image and to apply some basic distortion techniques. These commands can be accessed by selecting Image>Transform from the Menu bar.

Free Transform
This enables you to manually alter the size of an image. To do this:

1   Select Image>Transform>Free Transform from the Menu bar

2   Click OK if you are prompted to make the background a layer

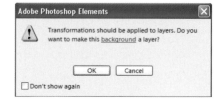

The other options from the Transform menu are Skew, Distort and Perspective. These can be applied in a similar way to the Free Transform option.

3   Click and drag here to transform the vertical size of the image

4   Click and drag here to transform the horizontal size of the image

5   Click and drag here to transform the vertical and horizontal size of the image. Hold down Shift to transform it in proportion

Magnification

There are a number of ways in Elements in which the magnification at which an image is being viewed can be increased or decreased. This can be useful if you want to zoom in on a particular part of an image, for editing purposes, or if you want to view a whole image to see the result of editing effects that have been applied.

View menu

1 Select View from the Menu bar and select one of the options from the View menu

Zoom tool

1 Select the Zoom tool from the Toolbox:

2 Click once on an image to enlarge it (usually by 100% each time). Hold down Alt and click to decrease the magnification

Navigator palette

This can be used to move around an image and also magnify certain areas. To use the Navigator palette:

1 Click and drag here to detach the Navigator palette from the palette bin

2 Drag this slider to magnify the area of the image within the red rectangle

The Navigator palette also has buttons for zooming in and out. These are located at the left and right of the slider.

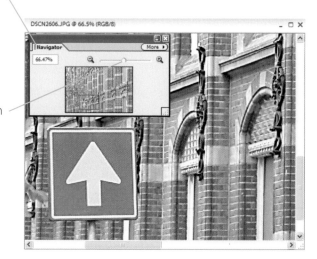

3 Drag the rectangle to change the area of the image that is being magnified

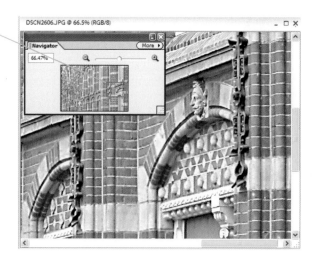

Burn and dodge

Burn and dodge are two traditional photographic techniques for darkening (burn) or lightening (dodge) areas of an image. In Elements there are tools in the Toolbox for achieving these effects. To do this:

1 Open the original image

The Burn and Dodge tools can be used on a whole image, or a selection can be made within the image and the tools used within the selection. In this case, only the pixels within the selected area will be affected by the tools.

2 Select the Burn tool from the Toolbox and drag it over an area of the image to darken it

Options for the Burn and Dodge tools can be selected on the Options bar once the tools have been selected.

3 Select the Dodge tool from the Toolbox and drag it over an area of the image to lighten it

Sponge

The Sponge tool is used in a similar way to the Burn and Dodge tools, except that it increases or decreases the color saturation of the area over which it is applied. To use the Sponge tool:

1   Select the Sponge tool in the Toolbox and click here in the Options bar to select Saturate or Desaturate

2   Drag the Sponge tool over the image, or an area of the image, to achieve the desired effect

The saturation of a color is the intensity at which that color is displayed.

Eraser

The Eraser tool can be used to remove areas of an image. In a simple, single layer, image, this can just leave a blank hole, which has to be filled with something. A more artistic use of the Eraser tool can be made when an image consists of two or more layers. Areas of the top layer can then be erased, to achieve a more creative effect. To do this:

For more about working with layers, see Chapter Seven.

1 Open an image that consists of two or more layers

2 Select the Eraser tool from the Toolbox:

3 Drag the Eraser tool over part of the top layer in the image

4 The bottom layer is revealed through the erased area, creating an artistic effect with the two layers

Erasing a background

Another option for erasing is to remove the background of an image. This can be done with the Magic Eraser tool. It is possible to delete a colored background in an image, wherever it appears in the image. To do this:

1 Open an image with an evenly colored background

2 Select the Magic Eraser tool from the Toolbox and make the required selections in the Options bar. Make sure the Contiguous box is not checked

Tolerance: 50 ☑ Anti-alias ☐ Contiguous ☐ Sample All Layers | Opacity: 100% ▶

3 Click once on the background. It is removed from the image, regardless of where it occurs

Quick wins for digital images

In digital image editing, there are a number of techniques and effects that can be used to quickly and significantly enhance images. This chapter looks at some of these "quick wins" and shows how they can be applied to images.

Covers

Chapter Four

Removing red-eye

One of the most common problems with photographs of people, whether they are taken digitally or with a film-based camera, is red-eye. This is caused when the camera's flash is used and then reflects in the subject's pupils. This can create the dreaded red-eye effect, when the subject can unintentionally be transformed into a demonic character. Unless you have access to professional studio lighting equipment or have a removable flash unit that can be positioned away from the subject's face, sooner or later you will capture images that contain red-eye.

The best way to deal with red-eye is to avoid it in the first place. Try using a camera that has a red-eye reduction function. This uses an extra flash, just before the picture is taken, to diminish the effect of red-eye.

Elements has recognized that removing red-eye is one of the top priorities for most amateur photographers and a specific tool for this purpose has been included in the Toolbox: the Red Eye Removal tool. To use this:

Open an image that contains red-eye

2 Select the Zoom tool from the Toolbox:

3 Drag around the affected area until it appears at a suitable magnification

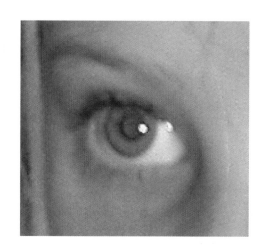

4 Select the Red Eye Removal tool from the Toolbox:

5 Click in the Options bar to select the size of the pupil and the amount by which it will be darkened

Red-eye can be removed by clicking near the affected area: it does not have to be directly on it.

6 Click once on the red-eye, or drag around the affected area

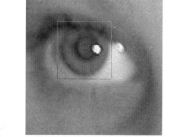

7 The red-eye is removed

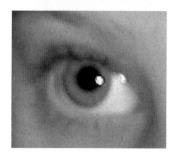

Removing red-eye in the Photo Browser

Red-eye can be removed from multiple images in a single operation, from within the Photo Browser. To do this:

1. Access the Photo Browser and select two or more images that contain red-eye

2. Select Edit>Auto Red Eye Fix Selected Photos from the Menu bar

To view all images in a version set, select it in the Photo Browser and select Edit> Version Set>Reveal Items in Version Set from the Menu bar.

3. The selected images have their red-eye removed automatically

4. The edited images are placed in a version set, with the original remaining intact and the edited image being the one without the red-eye

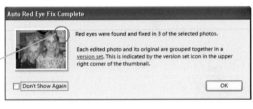

Auto Red Eye Fix Complete

Red eyes were found and fixed in 3 of the selected photos.

Each edited photo and its original are grouped together in a version set. This is indicated by the version set icon in the upper right corner of the thumbnail.

☐ Don't Show Again   OK

When removing red-eye automatically from images in the Photo Browser or the Photo Downloader, always check that the process has work satisfactorily and that you are happy with the result.

Removing red-eye when downloading

Red-eye can also be removed from images as they are downloaded from a digital device. To do this:

1. Access the Photo Downloader

2. Check this box to remove red-eye while images are being downloaded

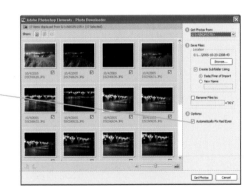

Adjusting skin tones

Skin tones can sometimes cause problems in digital images. At times they can look washed-out and pale or contain a slightly unnatural color cast. This can be edited with the Adjust Skin Tones function, which can be used to improve the skin tone of a pale image or just to give someone a more tanned or healthy appearance. To do this:

1 In the Editor, open an image whose skin tone you want to adjust

2 Select Enhance>Adjust Color>Adjust Color for Skin Tones from the Menu bar

It is best to make small adjustments when editing skin tones, otherwise the results can look too unnatural.

3 Click on the image to automatically adjust the skin tone in relation to the selected area

4 Drag these sliders to alter the amount of tan and blush in the skin tone

5 Drag this slider to edit the overall light in the image

6 Click OK

Straightening an image

If you use scanned images, you will quickly discover that it can be difficult to capture a perfectly straight image. Invariably, scanned images appear at a slight angle once the scanning process has been completed, however careful you are when you place the original image in the scanner. As shown in Chapter Three, images can be rotated manually, but there is also a function for straightening images in one operation. To straighten an image:

When scanning images it is best not to spend too much time trying to get the image straight. This is because it can be a frustrating process and also because of the ease with which Elements can cure the problem.

1 Open the image that requires to be straightened

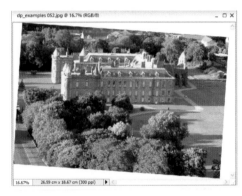

2 Select the Straighten tool from the Toolbox

Once they have been straightened images can also be cropped manually using the Crop tool in the Toolbox.

3 Drag on the image at the angle by which you want it to be straightened

Images can also be straightened by selecting Image>Rotate> Straighten and Crop Image from the Menu bar.

4 The image is straightened according to the angle used in Step 3

Dividing scanned images

Scanning is now a very popular way to capture digital images by converting existing hard copy photographs. Previously, each image had to be scanned individually, or several images could be scanned at the same time but they then had to be copied and cropped individually, which could be a tedious process. However, it is now possible to take the hard work out of dividing scanned images by letting Elements do it automatically. To do this:

1 Scan two, or more, images at the same time

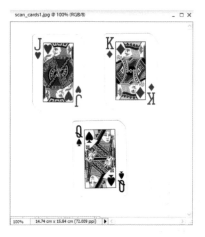

When scanning images to be divided, make sure that there is enough white space between them and that each image has a clearly defined border. This will enable Elements to clearly identify the separate images and then divide them.

2 Select Image>Divide Scanned Photos from the Menu bar

3 Each image is cropped and straightened and then saved into its own individual file

Quick Fix options

The Quick Fix options in Elements offer a number of functions within the one location. This makes it easier to apply a number of techniques at the same time.

Using Quick Fix

1. Open an image in the Editor and click here in the Shortcuts bar

2. Click here for options for how the image is displayed on screen

3. Click here for options for zooming, moving around the image, cropping and removing red-eye

Several options can be applied sequentially, without having to leave the Quick Fix dialog box. To do this, click the check mark in each palette after each effect has been selected.

4. Correction palettes are located here. Click a right-pointing arrow to expand a palette

5. Click here to specify how the editing changes are displayed

General Quick Fixes

To perform general orientation and color correction tasks with the Quick Fix option:

1 Click here to perform an Auto Smart Fix edit

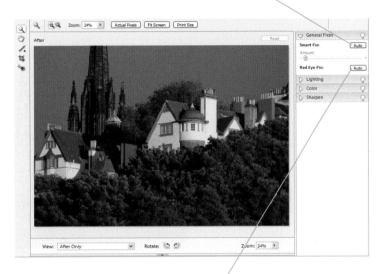

Changes are displayed in the main Quick Fix window as they are being made.

2 Click here to automatically remove red-eye

3 Drag this slider to manually edit the colors, shadows and highlights

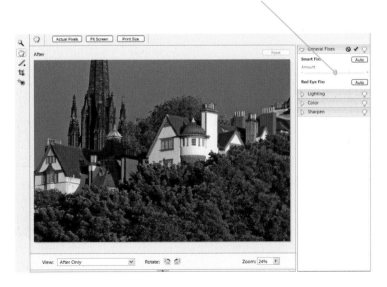

Lighting Quick Fixes

To improve the lighting and contrast in an image with the Quick Fix option:

1 Click here to automatically adjust the levels and contrast in an image

In general, when applying lighting fixes, it is more effective to apply them manually rather than using the Auto functions.

2 Drag these sliders to manually adjust the shadows, highlights and midtones in an image

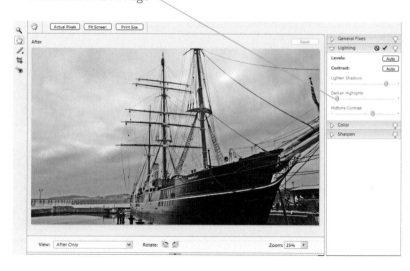

Color Quick Fixes

To improve the color in an image with the Quick Fix option:

1 Click here to automatically adjust the colors in an image

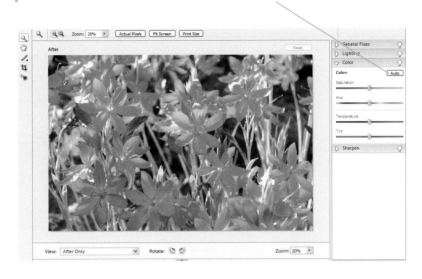

Extreme color corrections can result in some interesting artistic effects.

2 Drag these sliders to manually adjust the colors in an image

Sharpening Quick Fixes

To improve the definition in an image with the Quick Fix option:

1 Click here to automatically adjust the sharpness in an image

Sharpening works by emphasizing the edges between adjoining pixels in an image.

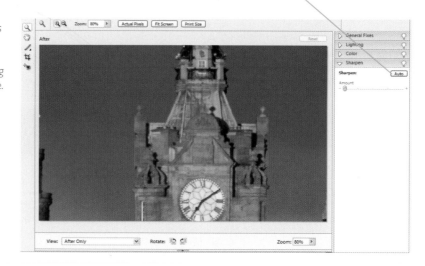

If too much sharpening is applied, the affected area could appear almost serrated since the lines between adjacent pixels will become too noticeable.

2 Drag this slider to manually adjust the sharpening in an image

When the Quick Fix editing has been completed, you can return to the main editing window by clicking the Standard Edit button on the Shortcuts bar.

Variations

The Variations option is a quick way to see how an image will look with varying amounts of different colors applied to it. To do this:

Color Variations can be used to correct images if too much of a particular color occurs in the image. This can happen if a digital camera does not record the color accurately when capturing an image.

1 Open an image in Editor mode and select Enhance>Adjust Color>Color Variations from the Menu bar

2 Select a color variation to use for the image. The selection is displayed in "After" at the top of the window

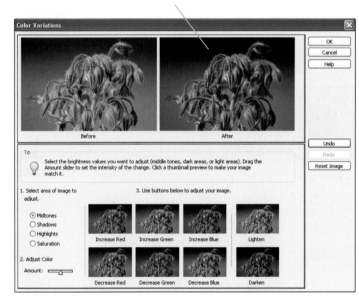

To apply a greater amount of each variation, click on the selected thumbnail several times.

3 Select an area of the image to adjust

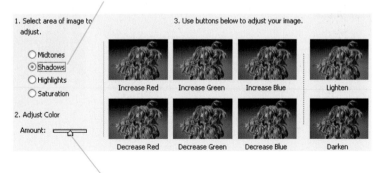

4 Drag this slider to alter the amount of the adjustment

Creating grayscale images

Most digital cameras and scanners are capable of converting color images into grayscale at the point of capture. However, it is also possible to use Elements to convert existing color images into grayscale ones. To do this:

The term "grayscale" refers to a range of gray shades between white and black.

1 Open a color image and select Image>Mode> Grayscale from the Menu bar

When creating grayscale images, make a copy of the original first. Use the copy to create the grayscale image.

2 In the subsequent dialog box, click OK to remove the color information from the image

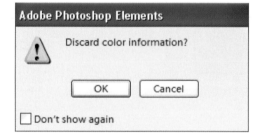

A similar effect can be achieved by selecting Enhance>Adjust Color>Remove Color from the Menu bar.

3 The image is converted into grayscale. Some color adjustment editing can then be done, such as Brightness/ Contrast

Panoramas

Creating panoramas

For anyone who takes landscape pictures, the desire to create a panorama occurs sooner or later. With film-based cameras, this usually involves sticking several photographs together to create the panorama, albeit a rather patchwork one. With digital images the end result can look a lot more professional and Elements has a dedicated function for achieving this: Photomerge.

When creating a panorama there are a few rules to follow:

Do not include too many images in a panorama, otherwise it could be too large for viewing or printing easily.

- If possible, use a tripod to ensure that your camera stays at the same level for all of the shots

- Keep the same exposure settings for all images

- Make sure that there is a reasonable overlap between images (about 20%). Some cameras enable you to align the correct overlap between the images

- Keep the same distance between yourself and the object you are capturing. Otherwise the end result will look out of perspective

To create a panorama:

Capture the images that you want to use in the panorama and open them in Editor mode

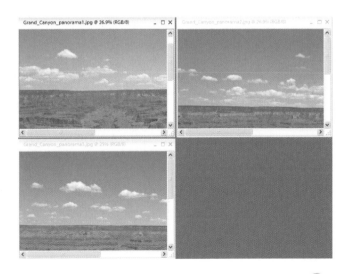

...cont'd

The tools at the top left of the Photomerge box can be used to (from top to bottom) Select, Rotate, Set Vanishing Point, Zoom or Move the panorama.

Click on the Cylindrical Mapping check box under Composition Settings to create a 3-D barrel effect for the panorama. This is only available if the Perspective radio button has been selected.

Click on the Advanced Blending box under Composition Settings to adjust any differences in exposure in the individual images.

2   Select File>New>Photomerge Panorama from the Menu bar

3   Click Browse to locate any more images you want to use. The images are displayed in the Source Files box. Click OK

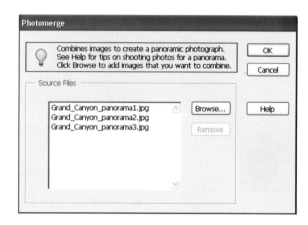

4   The panorama is created in the Photomerge dialog box. Click OK to create the panorama in Editor view

5 In some instances the image may need some additional editing. One common problem is the appearance of diagonal lines across the image, particularly in areas of sky

Panoramas do not just have to be of landscapes. They can also be used for items such as a row of buildings or crowds at a sporting event.

6 Panoramas can usually be improved by applying color correction such as Brightness/Contrast and Shadows/Highlights. They can also be cropped to straighten the borders

7 An unwanted line in a panorama can be removed by cloning from a nearby area or by selecting it and applying color correction until it is the same tone as the rest of the image

Non-sequential panoramas

Panoramas of images that are not in sequence are created in a similar way to sequential ones, except that the process is less automated. To create a non-sequential panorama, complete the first four steps for creating a panorama; then:

1   A warning box appears stating that the images cannot be created as a panorama. Click OK

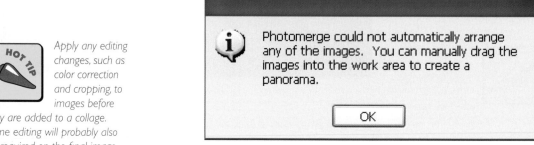

Apply any editing changes, such as color correction and cropping, to images before they are added to a collage. Some editing will probably also be required on the final image, but try and lessen the amount of work at this stage by preparing the images initially.

2   Drag the images into the Photomerge work area to combine them into a single image. Position them manually to create the required effect

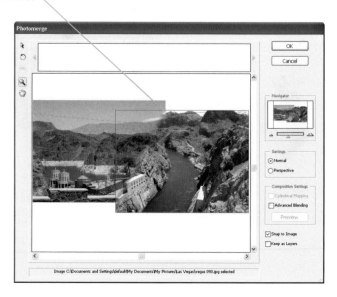

Beyond the basics

Since Elements is based on the full version of Photoshop, it contains a number of powerful features for precise image editing. This chapter looks at some of these features and shows how you can take your image editing skills to the next level.

Covers

Chapter Five

Hue and saturation

The hue and saturation command can be used to edit the color elements of an image. However, it works slightly differently from commands such as those for the brightness and contrast. There are three areas that are covered by the hue and saturation command: color, color strength and lightness. To adjust the hue and saturation of an image:

1   Open an image

2   Select Enhance>Adjust Color>Adjust Hue/Saturation

By altering the hue of an image some interesting abstract color effects can be created. This can be very effective if you are producing several versions of the same image, such as for a poster.

3   Drag this slider to adjust the hue of the image, i.e. change the colors in the image

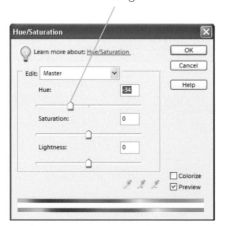

Hue is used to describe the color of a pixel or an image.

4 Drag this slider to adjust the saturation, i.e. the intensity of colors in the image

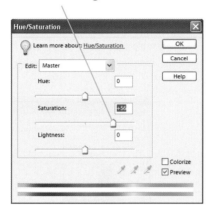

The Lightness option is similar to adjusting image brightness.

5 Check on the Colorize box to color the image with the hue of the currently selected foreground color in the Color Picker, which is located at the bottom of the Toolbox

The Colorize option can be used to create some interesting "color wash" effects. Try altering the Hue slider once the Colorize box has been checked.

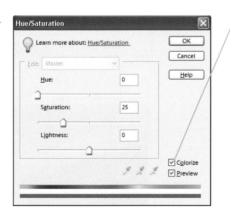

For more on working with color and the Color Picker, see Chapter Eight.

6 Click OK to apply any changes that have been made

Histogram

The histogram is a device that displays the tonal range of the pixels in an image and it can be used for very precise editing of an image. The histogram (Window>Histogram) is depicted in a graph format and it displays how the pixels in an image are distributed across the image, from the darkest (black) to the lightest (white) points. Another way of considering the histogram is that it displays the values of an image's highlights, midtones and shadows:

The histogram works by looking at the individual color channels of an image (Red, Green, Blue, also known as the RGB color model) or at a combination of all three, which is displayed as the Luminosity in the Channel box. It can also look at all of the colors in an image.

Highlights

Midtones

Shadows

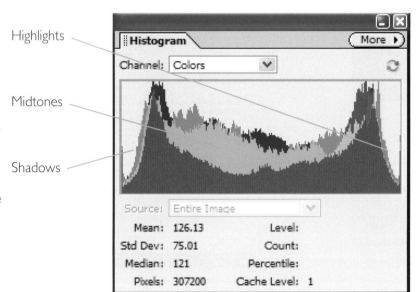

Image formats such as JPEG are edited in Elements using the RGB color model, i.e. red, green and blue mixed together to create the colors in the image.

Highlights

Midtones

Shadows

Ideally, the histogram graph should show a reasonably consistent range of tonal distribution, indicating an image that has good contrast and detail:

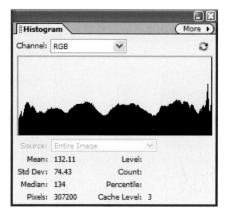

If the histogram is left open, it will update automatically as editing changes are made to an image. This gives a good idea of how effective the changes are.

However, if the tonal range is bunched at one end of the graph, this indicates that the image is underexposed or overexposed:

Overexposure

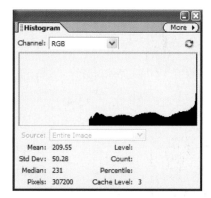

Underexposure

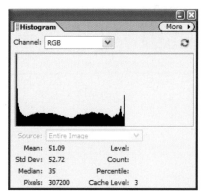

Levels

While the histogram displays the tonal range of an image, the Levels function can be used to edit this range. Any changes made using the Levels function will then be visible in the histogram. Levels allow you to redistribute pixels between the darkest and lightest points in an image, and also to set these points manually if you want to. To use the Levels function:

The Levels function can be used to adjust the tonal range of a specific area of an image by first making a selection and then using the Levels dialog box. For more details on selecting areas see Chapter Six.

In the Levels dialog box, the graph is the same as the one shown in the histogram.

Image shadows, midtones and highlights can be altered by dragging the markers for the black, midtone and white input points.

 Open an image

2 Select Enhance>Adjust Lighting>Levels from the Menu bar

Midtone input point

Black input point

White input point

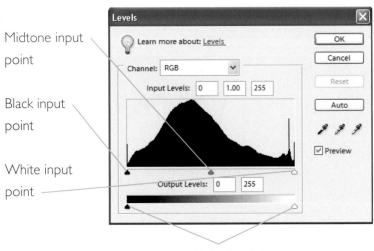

Output points

3 Drag the black point and the white point sliders to, or beyond, the first pixels denoted in the graph to increase the contrast

It is worth adjusting an image's black and white points before any other editing is performed.

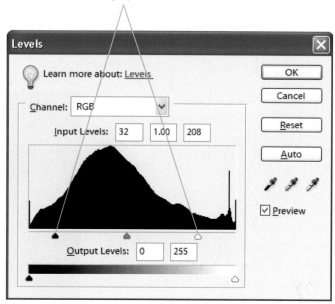

Move the midtones point slider to darken or lighten the midtones in an image.

4 Drag the output sliders towards the middle to decrease the contrast

The Auto button in the Levels dialog box produces the same effect as using the Enhance>Auto Levels command from the Menu bar.

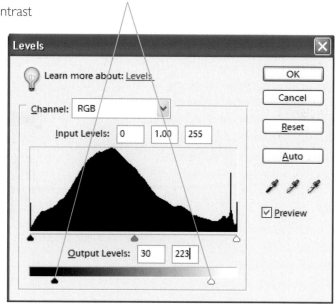

Adjusting levels with filters

It is also possible to adjust the levels in an image without changing anything in the original image. This is done by applying a filter on a separate layer above the main image, which then becomes a background layer. This is a useful technique as the levels can then be edited by changing the filter layer rather than the image itself. To adjust the levels in an image using a layers filter:

1 Open an image that is either too dark or too light

For more details about adjustment layers, see Chapter Seven.

2 Select Window>Layers from the Menu bar to access the Layers palette

3 Click here to access the adjustment layers options

4 Click here to select the levels filter

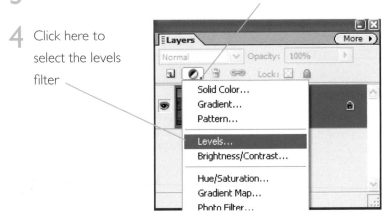

Editing the levels of an adjustment filter is just the same process as editing the levels of the image directly.

5 Make the required changes in the Levels dialog box and click OK

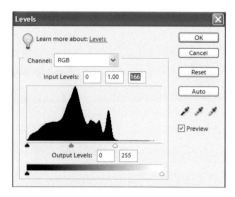

Using an adjustment layer to edit the levels in an image means that the levels can be edited further simply by editing the adjustment layer, since the image itself has not been touched. Alternatively, the adjustment layer can be deleted to revert to the original state of the image.

6 The levels filter is created on a layer above the background image, which is displayed here in the Layers palette

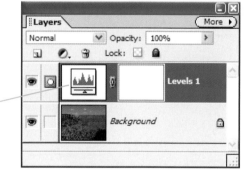

7 The exposure is improved, although the image itself is untouched. Double-click on the levels filter in the Layers palette to edit it

Pegging black and white points

Since Levels works by distributing pixels between the black and white points of an image, it makes sense to define these points for each image. This can be done by using the eyedroppers in the Levels dialog box:

1 With an image open, access the Levels dialog box by selecting Enhance>Adjust Lighting>Levels from the Menu bar

The Info palette can be used to see the color values of the areas selected for the black, white and gray points.

2 Click on the Set Black Point eyedropper and click on the image's darkest point to set the black point

To set a white point, use an area that is colored white, rather than a burnt out area of an image.

3 Click on the Set Gray Point eyedropper and click on a gray area to set the midtone point

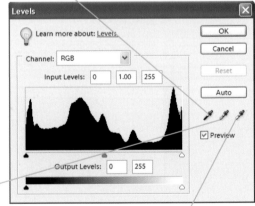

If the color in an image does not look right after setting the black, gray and white points, try selecting different areas of color with the relevant eyedroppers.

4 Click on the Set White Point eyedropper and click on the image's lightest point to set the white point

Equalize

The Equalize function works in a similar way to adjusting the Levels of an image, in that it redistributes the pixels in an image to try and achieve a more consistent level of brightness throughout the image. To equalize an image:

1 Open an image

2 Select Filter>Adjustments>Equalize from the Menu bar

3 Color is equalized across the image

Invert

The Invert function creates a negative effect for an image. To invert an image:

1 Open an image

The negative effect produced by the Invert function on a color image is not exactly the same as a film negative. However, if it is applied to a black and white image it is almost the same as a genuine black and white negative.

2 Select Filter>Adjustments>Invert from the Menu bar

3 The negative of the image is displayed

Posterize

The Posterize function reduces the number of colors used in an image, to create a more abstract appearance. To posterize an image:

1 Open an image

2 Select Filter>Adjustments>Posterize from the Menu bar

3 Enter a figure for the number of color levels to be used. Click OK

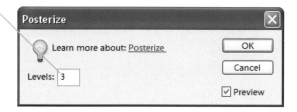

4 The number of color levels in the image is reduced accordingly

Sharpening

Sharpening is a technique that can be used to improve the definition of a slightly blurred image. It does this by emphasizing the contrast between adjacent pixels. The full range of sharpening options is available from the Filter>Sharpen menu on the Menu bar and there is also a Sharpen tool in the Toolbox. To use this:

1 Open an image that looks slightly blurry or fuzzy

2 Select the Sharpen tool in the Toolbox and make the required changes in the Options bar settings

Sharpening is useful for images that are going to be printed: it is more forgiving than viewing images online.

3 Drag the Sharpen tool over the image, or part of the image, to make it appear crisper

Unsharp Mask

Although sharpening is a useful technique for improving the overall definition of an image, it can sometimes appear too harsh and "jaggy". For a more subtle effect the Unsharp Mask can be used. This works by increasing the contrast between light and dark pixels in an image. To use the Unsharp Mask:

1 Open an image that you want to sharpen

2 Select Filter>Sharpen> Unsharp Mask from the Menu bar

The settings for the Unsharp Mask are: Amount, which determines the amount to increase the contrast between pixels; Radius, which determines how many pixels will have the sharpening applied to them in an affected area; and Threshold, which determines how different a pixel has to be from its neighbor before sharpening is applied.

3 Apply the appropriate settings in the Unsharp Mask dialog box and click OK

4 The contrast between light and dark pixels is increased, giving the impression of a clearer, or sharper, image

Image size

The physical size of a digital image can sometimes be a confusing issue as it is frequently dealt with under the term "resolution". Unfortunately, resolution can be applied to a number of areas of digital imaging: image resolution, monitor resolution, print size and print resolution.

Image resolution

The resolution of an image is determined by the number of pixels in it. This is counted as a vertical and a horizontal value, e.g. 640 x 480. When multiplied together it gives the overall resolution, i.e. 307,200 pixels in this case. This is frequently the headline figure quoted by digital camera manufacturers, e.g. 5 million pixels (or 5 megapixels). To view the image resolution in Elements:

To view an image on a monitor at its actual size or the size at which it will currently be printed, select the Zoom tool from the Toolbox and select Actual Pixels or Print Size from the Options bar.

1 Select Image> Resize>Image Size from the Menu bar

2 The image size is displayed here (in pixels)

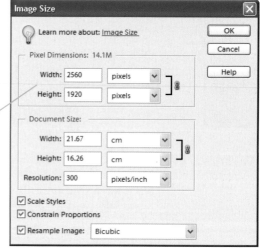

The Resolution figure under the Document Size heading is used to determine the size at which the image will be printed. If this is set to 72, then the onscreen size and the printed size should be roughly the same.

Monitor resolution

Most modern computer monitors display digital images at between 72 and 96 pixels per inch (ppi). This means that every inch of the screen contains approximately this number of pixels. So for an image being displayed at 100%, the onscreen size will be the number of pixels horizontally divided by 72 (or 96 depending on the monitor) and the same vertically. In the above example this would mean the image would be viewed at 9 inches by 6.5 inches approximately.

Document size (print resolution)

Pixels in an image are not a set size, which means that images can be printed at a variety of sizes, simply by contracting or expanding the available pixels. This is done by changing the resolution in the Document Size section of the Image Size dialog box. (When dealing with document size, think of this as the size of the printed document.) To set the size at which an image will be printed:

The higher the print resolution, the better the final printed image. Aim for a minimum of 200 pixels per inch for the best printed output.

To work out the size at which an image will be printed, divide the pixel dimensions (height and width) by the resolution value under the Document Size heading.

The print resolution determines how many pixels are used in each inch of the printed image. However, the number of colored dots used to represent each pixel on the paper is determined by the printer resolution, measured in dots per inch (dpi). So if the print resolution is 72 ppi and the printer resolution is 2880 dpi, each pixel will be represented by 40 colored dots, i.e. 2880 divided by 72.

1 Select Image>Resize>Image Size from the Menu bar

2 Change the resolution here (or change the Width and Height of the document size). Make sure the Resample Image box is not checked

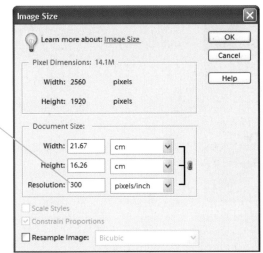

3 By changing one value, the other two are updated automatically. Click OK

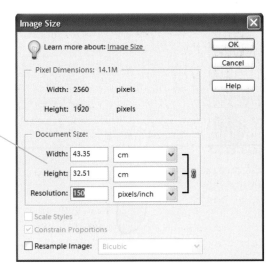

Resampling images

All digital images can be increased or decreased in size. This involves adding or removing pixels from the image. Decreasing the size of an image is relatively straightforward and involves removing redundant pixels. However, increasing the size of an image involves adding pixels by digital guesswork. To do this, Elements looks at the existing pixels and works out the nearest match for the ones that are to be added. Increasing or decreasing the size of a digital image is known as "resampling".

The process of adding pixels to an image to increase its size is known as "interpolation".

Resampling

Resampling down decreases the size of the image and it is more effective than resampling up. To do this:

Since it involves digital guesswork by Elements, resampling up results in inferior image quality.

1 Select Image> Resize>Image Size from the Menu bar

To keep the same resolution for an image, resample it by changing the pixel dimensions' height and width. To keep the same Document Size (i.e. the size at which it will be printed) resample it by changing the resolution.

2 Check the Resample Image box

3 Resample the image by changing the pixel dimensions, the height and width or the resolution

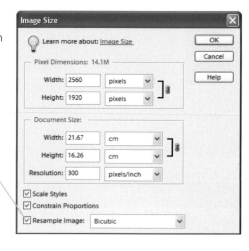

4 Changing any of the values above alters the physical size of the image. Click OK

Make sure the Constrain Proportions box is checked if you want the image to be increased or decreased in size proportionally, rather than just one value being altered.

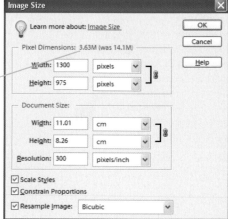

Selecting areas

The true power of digital image editing comes into its own when you are able to select areas of an image and edit them independently from the rest of the image. This chapter looks at the various ways that selections can be made with Elements and shows how to edit individual selections.

Covers

Chapter Six

About selections

One of the most important aspects of image editing is the ability to select areas within an image. This can be used in a number of different ways:

- Selecting an object to apply an editing technique to it (such as changing the brightness or contrast) without affecting the rest of the image

- Selecting a particular color in an image

- Selecting an area to apply a special effect to it

- Selecting an area to remove it

Elements has several tools that can be used to select items and there are also a number of editing functions that can be applied to selections.

Two examples of how selections can be used are:

Once a selection has been made it stays selected even when another tool is activated, to allow for editing to take place.

1 Select an area within an image and delete it

The best way to deselect a selection is to click on it once with one of the selection tools, preferably the one used to make the selection.

2 Select an area and add a color or special effect

Marquee tools

There are two options for the Marquee tool: the Rectangular Marquee tool and the Elliptical Marquee tool. Both of these can be used to make symmetrical selections. To use the Marquee tools:

To access additional tools from the Toolbox, click and hold on the black triangle next to one of the default tools and select one of the subsequent options that are available.

1 Select either the Rectangular or the Elliptical Marquee tool from the Toolbox. Select the required options from the Options bar

2 Make a symmetrical selection with one of the tools by clicking and dragging on an image

To make a selection that is exactly square or round, hold down Shift when dragging with the Rectangular Marquee tool or the Elliptical Marquee tool respectively.

Elliptical selection   Rectangular selection

Lasso tools

There are three options for the Lasso tools, which can be used to make freehand selections. To use these:

Lasso tool

| Select the Lasso tool from the Toolbox and select the required options from the Options bar

When a selection has been completed (i.e. its end point reaches its start point), a small circle will appear at the side of whichever Lasso tool is being used. Click at this point to complete the selection.

2 Make a freehand selection by clicking and dragging around an object

Polygonal Lasso tool

Making a selection with the Polygonal Lasso tool is like creating a dot-to-dot pattern.

| Select the Polygonal Lasso tool from the Toolbox and select the required options from the Options bar

2 Make a selection by clicking on specific points around an object and then dragging to the next point

Magnetic Lasso tool

1 Select the Magnetic Lasso tool from the Toolbox and select the required options from the Options bar

On the Options bar for the Magnetic Lasso tool, the Edge Contrast value determines the amount of contrast there has to be between two colors for the selection line to snap to them. A high value detects lines with a high contrast and vice versa.

2 Click once on an image to create the first anchor point

The Frequency setting on the Options bar determines how quickly the fastening points are inserted as a selection is being made. A high value places the fastening points more quickly than a low value.

3 Make a selection by dragging continuously around an object. The selection line snaps to the closest strongest edge, i.e. the one with the most contrast. Fastening points are added as the selection is made

Magic Wand tool

The Magic Wand tool can be used to select areas of the same, or similar, color. To do this:

On the Options bar for the Magic Wand tool, the Tolerance box determines the range of colors that will be selected in relation to the color you click on. A low value will only select a very narrow range of colors in relation to the initially selected one, while a high value will include a greater range. The values range from 0–255.

1. Select the Magic Wand tool from the Toolbox and select the required options from the Options bar

2. Click on a color to select all of the adjacent pixels that are the same, or similar, color, depending on the options selected from the Options bar

On the Options bar for the Magic Wand tool, check the Contiguous box to ensure that only adjacent colors are selected. To select the same, or similar, color throughout the image, whether adjacent or not, uncheck the Contiguous box.

Selection Brush tool

The Selection Brush tool can be used to select areas by using a brush-like stroke. Unlike with the Marquee or Lasso tools, the area selected by the Selection Brush tool is the one directly below where the tool moves. To make a selection with the Selection Brush tool:

1. Select the Selection Brush tool from the Toolbox and select the required options from the Options bar

The Selection Brush tool can be used to select an area or to mask an area. This can be determined in the Mode box in the Options bar.

2. Click and drag to make a selection

3. The selection area is underneath the borders of the Selection Brush tool

Magic Extractor tool

A popular editing technique for digital images is taking part of an image and placing it in another image. This is frequently done with images of people, to create interesting or humorous collages. The Magic Extractor tool aids this process by making it as easy as possible to remove an object in an image from its surrounding background. The extracted part of the image can then be copied and pasted into another image. To do this:

1. Open an image in the Editor and select Image>Magic Extractor from the Menu bar

The default colors for selecting the foreground and the background are red and blue respectively. However, these can be changed by clicking on their colors in the Tool Options area.

2. Click here to select the foreground selection brush. Click or scribble on areas you want to be included as the foreground

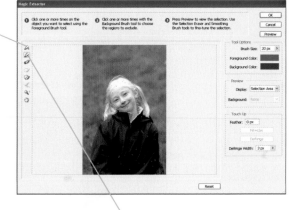

3. Click here to select the background selection brush and select the background in the same way as the foreground

4. Click Preview to see the selection effect

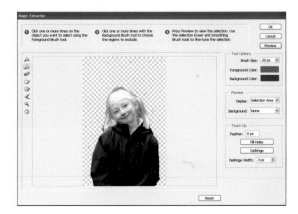

Use the zoom tool to get closer to areas that need to have parts of them deleted from the selection.

5 Click here and drag over any areas that have not been removed by the Magic Extractor tool

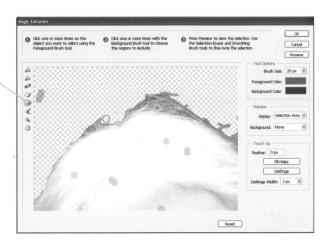

Once a subject has been extracted it can be copied from the original image file by first selecting it with the Move tool and then selecting Edit>Copy from the Menu bar.

6 Click OK

7 The selected item is available in the original image file

8 Select the extracted element and select Edit>Copy from the Menu bar

When an extracted object is pasted into another image it can be resized by dragging on the resizing handles in the same way as for any other selection.

9 Open a new image and select Edit>Paste from the Menu bar to insert the extracted element

Magic Selection Brush tool

A similar selection method to the Magic Extractor is the Magic Selection Brush. The difference is that it only selects one object, as opposed to both the foreground and the background. The Magic Selection Brush tool can be used to select an object quickly by scribbling on it or entering dots within the object. To do this:

1 Select the Magic Selection Brush tool from the Toolbox

2 Click here to select a color for the selection

When using the Magic Selection Brush tool, make sure that there is a good contrast between the area being selected and the rest of the image. Otherwise, unwanted areas of the image may become selected too.

3 Scribble on the object to be selected. The lines do not have to be accurate but they should cover all of the colors and tones of the target object

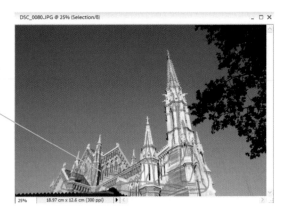

4 Release the mouse and the object becomes selected. Editing changes can now be applied to the selected object

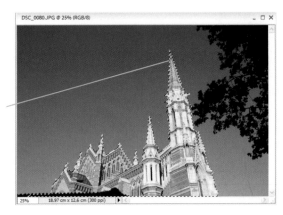

Defringing selections

The ability to select items within images means that they can then be pasted into other images to create composite images. However, one problem with this can be that the selected item has a slight halo effect as a result of additional, unwanted pixels being included along the edge of the selection. When it is pasted against a differently colored background these pixels show up as a thin line. This can be rectified using the defringe option. To do this:

1 Open an image in the Editor and make a selection against a colored background. Select Edit>Copy from the Menu bar

The halo effect is usually created by a border of only one or two pixels. However, if the selection is pasted onto a differently colored background this can result in a very noticeable unwanted line around the selection.

2 Open a new image and select Edit>Paste from the Menu bar. Some of the background from the first image may appear along the edge of the pasted item

3 Select Enhance>Adjust Color>Defringe Layer from the Menu bar

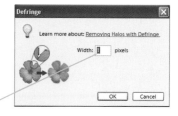

4 Enter the width of border by which you want the image defringed

5 Click OK

6 The halo effect is removed from the border

Inverting a selection

This can be a useful option if you have edited a selection and then you want to edit the rest of the image without affecting the area you have just selected. To do this:

1 Make a selection

2 Choose Select>Inverse from the Menu bar

When inverting a selection, ensure that the whole of the required area has been selected. If not, hold down Shift and make another selection to add this to the existing one.

3 The selection becomes inverted, i.e. if a background object was selected the foreground is now selected

Feathering

Feathering is a technique that can be used to soften the edges of a selection by making them slightly blurry. This can be used if you are pasting a selection into another image or if you want to soften the edges around a portrait of an individual. To do this:

Feathering can also be selected from the Options bar once a Marquee tool is selected and before the selection has been made.

1 Make a selection

2 Choose Select>Feather from the Menu bar

3 Enter a Feather value (the number of pixels around the radius of the selection that will be blurred). Click OK

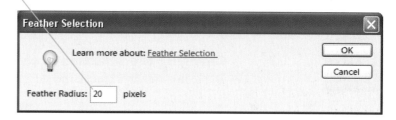

4 Invert the selection as shown on the previous page and delete the background by pressing Delete. This will leave the selection around the subject with softened edges

If required, crop the final image so that the feathered subject is more prominent.

Editing selections

When you've made a selection, you can edit it in a number of ways.

Moving

To move a selected area:

Once an area has been moved and deselected, it cannot then be selected independently again, unless it has been copied and pasted onto another layer.

1 Make a selection and select the Move tool from the Toolbox:

2 Drag the selection to move it to a new location

To deselect a selection, click once inside the selection area with the tool that was used to make the selection.

Changing the selection area

To change the area under the selection:

1 Make a selection with a selection tool

When changing the selection area, make sure that the New selection button is selected in the Options bar.

2 With the same tool selected, click and drag within the selection area to move it over another part of the image

Adding to a selection

To add to an existing selection:

1 Make a selection and click here in the Options bar

2 Make another selection to create a single, larger, selection. The two selections do not have to intersect

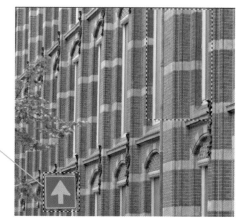

Intersecting with a selection

To create a selection by intersecting two existing selections:

1 Make a selection and click here in the Options bar

2 Make another selection that intersects the first. The intersected area will become the selection

Expanding a selection

To expand a selection by a specific number of pixels:

1. Make a selection and choose Select>Modify>Expand from the Menu bar

2. In the Expand Selection dialog box, enter the amount by which you want the selection expanded. Click OK

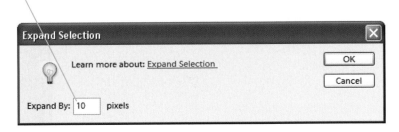

Growing a selection

The Grow command can be used on a selection when it has been made with the Magic Wand tool and some of the pixels within the selection have been omitted, due to being outside the tolerance. To do this:

1. Make a selection with the Magic Wand tool and make the required choices from the Options bar. Choose Select>Grow from the Menu bar

2. Depending on the choices in the Options bar, the omitted pixels are included in the selection and it has been expanded

Layers

For the artistically-minded who want to create more complex designs and effects with their images, the concept of layers is an invaluable one. It provides the means to add numerous elements to an image and edit them independently from one another. This chapter looks at how to use layers and also how they can be utilized to create fill effects and adjustment effects that can be applied without altering the original image.

Covers

Chapter Seven

Layering images

Layering is a technique that enables you to add additional elements to an image and place them on separate layers so that they can be edited and manipulated independently from other elements in the image. It is like creating an image using transparent sheets of film: each layer is independent of the others but, when they are combined, a composite image is created. This is an extremely versatile technique for working with digital images.

By using layers, several different elements can be combined to create a composite image:

Layers should usually be used when you are adding content to an image as this gives more flexibility for working with the various image elements.

Original image

Final image, with text and a shape added (two additional layers have been added)

Layers palette

The use of layers within Elements is governed by the Layers palette. When an image is first opened it is shown in the Layers palette as the Background layer. While this remains as the Background layer it cannot be moved above any other layers. However, it can be converted into a normal layer, in which case it operates in the same way as any other layers. To convert a Background layer into a normal one:

The Background layer can also be converted into a normal one by applying certain editing functions to the image. These are the Background Eraser tool, the Magic Eraser tool and the Red Eye Removal tool.

1 The open image is shown here in the Layers palette as the Background

2 Double-click here

3 Enter a name for the layer and click OK

The Layers palette menu can be accessed by clicking on the More button in the Layers palette.

4 The layer is converted into a normal layer in the Layers palette

Adding layers

New blank layers can be added whenever you want to include new content within an image. This could be part of another image that has been copied and pasted, a whole new image, text or an object. To add a new layer:

1 Click here on the Layers palette

Text is automatically added on a new layer and it is usually the topmost layer in an image.

2 Double-click here and overtype to give the layer a specific name

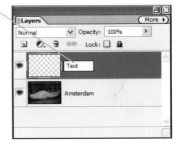

To edit an item on a particular layer, first make sure that the correct layer is selected in the Layers palette. A selected layer is known as the active layer and it is highlighted in the Layers palette with a solid color through it.

3 With the new layer selected in the Layers palette, add content to the layer. This will be visible over the layer, or layers, below it

Fill layers

Fill layers can be added to images to give a gradient or solid color effect behind or above the main subject. To do this:

1 Open the Layers palette and select a layer. The fill layer will be placed directly above the selected layer

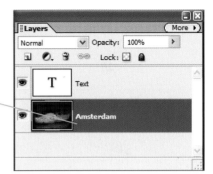

For the Fill layer to be visible behind the main image, the image must have a transparent background. To achieve this, select the main subject. Choose Select>Inverse from the Menu bar and press the Delete key to delete the background. A checkerboard effect should be visible, which denotes that this part of the image is transparent. This only works on layers that have been converted into normal layers, rather than the Background layer.

2 Click here at the top of the Layers palette

3 Select one of the fill options

Solid Color...
Gradient...
Pattern...

The Solid Color and Pattern options for fill layers both have their own dialog boxes and can be added in a similar way to the gradient option.

4 For a Gradient Fill, click here to select a gradient style and click OK

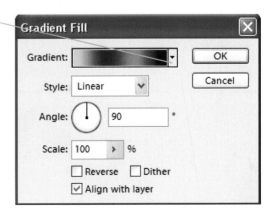

5 The fill layer appears above the layer that was initially selected

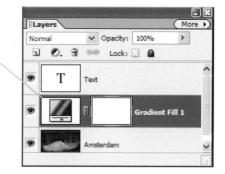

6 The fill layer covers everything below it. However, layers above it are still visible

If you want to edit a Fill or Adjustment layer, double-click on its icon in the Layer palette and then apply the required changes. To change the type of layer, select Layer> Change Layer Content from the Menu bar and select the new attributes for the layer.

7 Click here in the Layers palette and drag the slider to alter the opacity of the fill layer

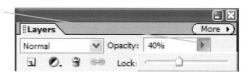

8 Once the opacity is altered, the layers below the fill layer are now visible, creating an artistic effect

Adjustment layers

Adjustment layers can be used to apply common color editing techniques, such as brightness and contrast, to an image without affecting the image itself, or any items above the Adjustment layer. The adjustment effect is added to a layer, which allows the image below to be viewed through this layer. To do this:

1 Open an image and click here on the Layers palette

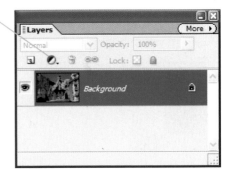

Adjustment layers affect any visible content on all of the layers below them, not just the one immediately below.

2 Select one of the adjustment options

Levels...
Brightness/Contrast...

Hue/Saturation...
Gradient Map...
Photo Filter...

Invert
Threshold...
Posterize...

3 Make editing changes for the selected adjustment item (in this example it is the Hue/Saturation). Click OK

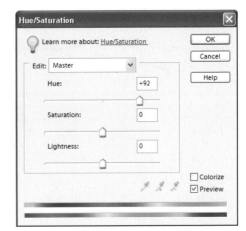

4 The effect in the Adjustment layer covers all of the layers below it. However, the layers themselves are unaltered

Although the Adjustment layer looks as if it has altered the image below it, it is in fact sitting above the image and has not affected it at all.

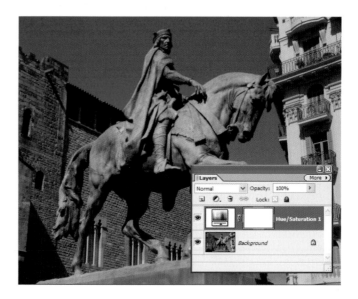

5 If content is added on layers above the Adjustment layer, this will be unaffected by the settings in the Adjustment layer

Both Fill and Adjustment layers are layer masks. This is a technique that enables the effect to be visible through the area of the mask.

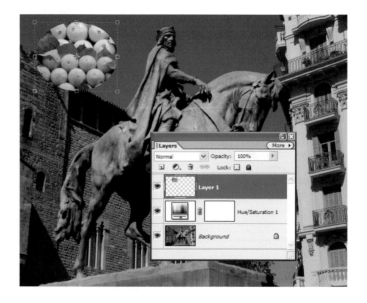

Working with layers

Moving layers

The order in which layers are arranged in the Layers palette is known as the stacking order. It is possible to change a layer's position in the stacking order, which affects how it is viewed in the composite image. To do this:

Click and drag a layer within the Layers palette to change its stacking order

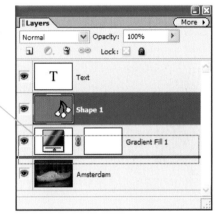

Layers can be deleted by selecting them and clicking on the Wastebasket icon in the Layers palette. However, this also deletes all of the content on that layer.

Hiding layers

Layers can be hidden while you are working on other parts of an image. However, the layer is still part of the composite image – it has not been removed. To hide a layer:

Click here so that the eye icon disappears. Click again to reveal it

Locking layers

Layers can be locked so that they cannot accidentally be edited while you are working on other parts of an image. To do this:

Select a layer and click here so that a padlock appears next to it

Blending layers

Blending is a technique that enables two layers to interact with each other in a variety of ways. To do this:

1. Select a layer either in the Layers palette or by clicking on the relevant item within an image

There are over twenty blend options. Experiment with them to see what effects they create.

2. Click here on the Layers palette

3. Select a blend option

4. The selected blend option determines how the selected layer interacts with the one below it

Opacity

The opacity of a layer can be set to determine how much of the layer below is visible through the selected layer. To do this:

1 Select a layer either in the Layers palette or by clicking on the relevant item within an image

Opacity is a good technique for creating a watermark effect. To do this, create a layer above the Background layer and set it to an opacity of approximately 20%–30%.

2 Click here and drag the slider to achieve the required level of opacity. The greater the amount of opacity, the less transparent the selected layer becomes

3 The opacity setting determines how much of the layer below is visible through the selected one and this can be used to create some interesting artistic effects

Saving layers

Once an image has been created using two or more layers there are two ways in which the composite image can be saved: in a proprietary Photoshop format, in which case individual layers are maintained, or in a general file format, in which case all of the layers will be merged into a single one. The advantage of the former is that individual elements can still be edited within the image, independently of other items. In general, it is good practice to save layered images in both a Photoshop and a non-Photoshop format. To save layered images in a Photoshop format:

1 Select File>Save As from the Menu bar

Before a layer is saved it is possible to create a composite image consisting of a single layer. To do this, select Layer>Flatten Image from the Menu bar. To merge the existing layer and the one below it, select Layer>Merge Down from the Menu bar and to merge all visible content (excluding any layers that have been hidden) select Layer> Merge Visible.

2 Make sure Photoshop (*.PSD, *.PDD) is selected as the format

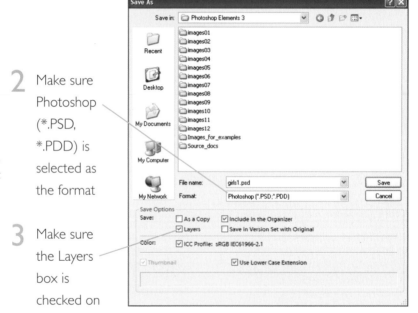

3 Make sure the Layers box is checked on

Layered images that are saved in the Photoshop PSD/PDD format can increase dramatically in file size compared with the original image, or a layered image that has been flattened.

4 Click Save

To save in a non-Photoshop format, select File>Save As from the Menu bar. Select the file format from the Format box and click OK. The Layers box will not be available.

Text and drawing objects

Elements offers a lot more than just the ability to edit digital images. It also has options for adding and formatting text and creating a variety of graphical objects. This chapter looks at how to add these items and also edit them using the drawing tools that are available.

Covers

Chapter Eight

Adding and formatting text

Text can be added to images in Elements and this can be used to create a wide range of items such as cards, brochures and posters. To add text to an image:

1 Select the Horizontal or Vertical Type tool from the Toolbox:

Use the Vertical Type tool sparingly as this is not a natural way for the eye to read text. Use it with small amounts of text, for effect.

2 Drag on the image with the Type tool to create a text box

3 Make the required formatting selections from the Options bar:

Anti-aliasing is a technique that smooths out the jagged edges that can sometimes appear with text when viewed on a computer monitor. Anti-aliasing is created by adding pixels to the edges of text so that it blends more smoothly with the background.

Font type   Font style   Font size   Anti-aliased

Formatting (bold, italic, underline and strikethrough)

Alignment   Spacing   Color   Orientation   Cancel

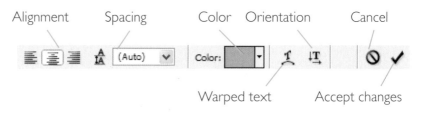

Warped text   Accept changes

4 Type the text onto the image. This is automatically placed on a new layer at the top of the stacking order in the Layers palette

5 To move the text, select it with the Move tool and click and drag it to a new position

To format text that has already been entered

1 Select a Type tool and drag it over a piece of text to select it

Vegas at night

2 Make the changes in the Options bar as shown in Step 3 on the facing page

Distorting text

In addition to producing standard text, it is also possible to create some dramatic effects by distorting text. To do this:

It is possible to select the distort options before text is added.

1 Enter plain text and select it by dragging a Type tool over it

2 Click the Create Warped Text button on the Options bar

3 Click here and select one of the options in the Warp Text dialog box. Click OK

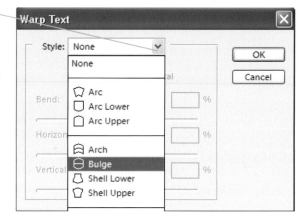

Use text distortion sparingly as it can become annoying if it is overdone.

4 The selected effect is applied to the text

Text and shape masks

Text masks can be used to reveal an area of an image showing through the text. This can be used to produce eye-catching headings and slogans. To do this:

1 Select the Horizontal or the Vertical Type Mask tool from the Toolbox:

T	Horizontal Type Tool	T
T	Vertical Type Tool	T
	Horizontal Type Mask Tool	T
	Vertical Type Mask Tool	T

2 Click on an image and enter and format text as you would for normal text. A red mask is applied to the image when the mask text is entered

Text mask effects work best if the text used is fairly large in size. In some cases it is a good idea to use bold text, as this is wider than standard text.

3 Press Enter or click the Move tool to border the mask text with dots

4 Select Edit>Copy from the Menu bar

5 Select File>New from the Menu bar and create a new file

Once a text mask has been copied it can also be pasted into other types of documents such as Word and desktop publishing documents.

6 Select Edit>Paste from the Menu bar to paste the text mask into the new file

Cookie Cutter masks

A similar effect can be created with shape masks by using the Cookie Cutter tool:

1 Select the Cookie Cutter tool in the Toolbox and click here to select a particular style in the Options bar

2 Drag on an image to create a cut-out effect

Adding shapes

Another way to add extra style to your images is through the use of shapes. There are several types of symmetrical shapes that can be added to images and also a range of custom ones. To add shapes to an image:

1 Click and hold the Rectangle tool in the Toolbox

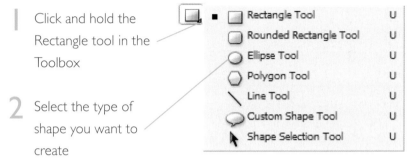

The tools for creating shapes are also available from the Options bar when the Rectangle tool (or any related tool) is selected.

2 Select the type of shape you want to create

3 Click and drag on the image to create the selected shape

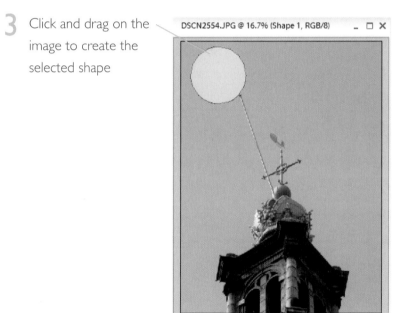

4 If you want to change the color of a shape, click here in the Options bar and select a new color. This can either be done before the shape is created or it can be used to edit the color of an existing shape, when selected with the Move tool

Custom shapes

Custom shapes can be used to add pre-designed graphical objects rather than just symmetrical shapes. To do this:

1 Select the Custom Shape tool from the Toolbox:

2 Click here in the Options bar to view the different custom shapes

3 Click once on a shape to select it

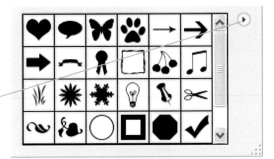

4 Click here to view other categories of shapes

5 Click and drag on an image to add a custom shape

Layer Styles

When plain text and objects are added to images, they appear as two-dimensional items. If you want to give them a 3-D effect, this can be achieved through the use of the Styles and Effects palette.

To do this:

Layer Styles can be applied to symmetrical objects and also custom ones.

1   Select Window>Styles and Effects from the Menu bar

2   Click here to access the Layer Styles

3   Click here to access different styles

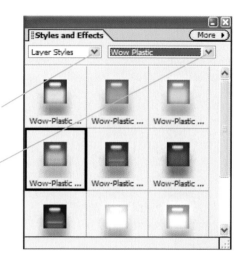

The Drop Shadow styles are a good option for adding emphasis to textual items such as headings. However, don't overuse them.

4   Select an object or a piece of text with the Move tool and click once on a layer style to apply that style to the selected item in the image

Paint Bucket tool

The Paint Bucket tool can be used to add a solid color to a selection or an object. To do this:

1 Select an area within an image or select an object

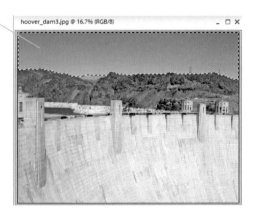

2 Select the Paint Bucket tool from the Toolbox:

For more information on working with color, see pages 143–144.

3 Click here in the Toolbox to access the Color Picker for changing the currently selected color

4 Click once on the selected area or object to change its color to the one loaded in the Paint Bucket tool

Gradient tool

The Gradient tool can be used to add a gradient fill to a selection or an object. To do this:

1 Select an area in an image or select an object

Copy of vegas 032.jpg @ 16.7% (RGB/8)

2 Select the Gradient tool from the Toolbox:

3 Click here in the Options bar to select preset gradient fills

Edit

4 Click on a gradient style to apply it as the default

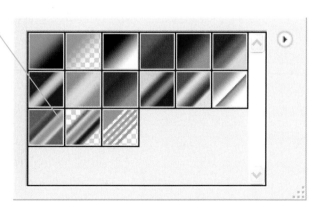

...cont'd

5 Click here in the Options bar to access the Gradient Editor dialog box

To create a new preset gradient, create it in the Gradient Editor dialog box and click on the New button to add it to the list of preset gradients. Double-click on the gradient's icon to give it a name in the Gradient Name dialog box.

6 Click and drag the sliders to change the amount of a particular color in the gradient

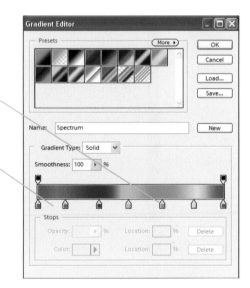

7 Click along here to add a new color marker. Click OK

The amount that the cursor is dragged when adding a gradient determines where the centerpoint of the gradient is located and also the size of each segment of the gradient.

8 Click an icon in the Options bar to select a gradient style

9 Click and drag within the original selection to specify the start and end points of the gradient effect

Brush and Pencil tools

The Brush and Pencil tools work in a similar way and can be used to create lines of varying thickness and style. To do this:

1 Select the Brush tool or the Pencil tool from the Toolbox:

2 Select the required options from the Options bar

The Mode options for the Brush and Pencil tools are similar to those for blending layers together. They include options such as Darken, Lighten, Soft Light and Difference. Each of these enables the line to blend with the image below it.

Size: 45 px Mode: Normal Opacity: 100%

3 Click and drag to create lines on an image. (The lines are placed directly on the image. To add lines without altering the background image, add a new layer above the background and add the lines on this layer. They will then be visible over the background.)

The Brush and Pencil tools are very similar in the way they function, except that the Brush tool has more options and can create more subtle effects.

DSCN2521.JPG @ 25% (RGB/8)

Impressionist Brush tool

The Impressionist Brush tool can be used to create a dappled effect over an image, similar to an impressionist painting. To do this:

If the Impressionist Brush tool is not visible in the Toolbox, click and hold on the black triangle next to the Brush tool and select it from the menu.

1 Select the Impressionist Brush tool from the Toolbox:

2 Select the required options from the Options bar

3 Click and drag over an image to create an impressionist effect

If the brush size is too large for the Impressionist Brush tool, it can result in the effect being too extreme and a lot of an image's definition being lost.

Working with color

All of the text and drawing tools make extensive use of color. Elements provides a number of methods for selecting colors and also for working with them.

Foreground and background colors

At the bottom of the Toolbox there are two colored squares. These represent the currently selected foreground and background colors. The foreground color, which is the most frequently used, is the one that is applied to drawing objects, such as fills and lines, and also text. The background color is used for items such as gradient fills and for areas that have been removed with the Eraser tool.

Foreground color   Swap foreground and background colors

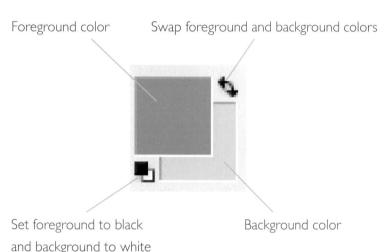

Whenever the foreground or background color squares are clicked on, the Eyedropper tool is automatically activated. This can be used to select a color, from anywhere on your screen, instead of using the Color Picker.

Set foreground to black   Background color
and background to white

Color Picker

The Color Picker can be used to select a new color for the foreground or background color. To do this:

Click once on the foreground or the background color square, as required

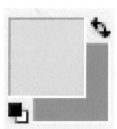

2 In the Color Picker, click to select a color

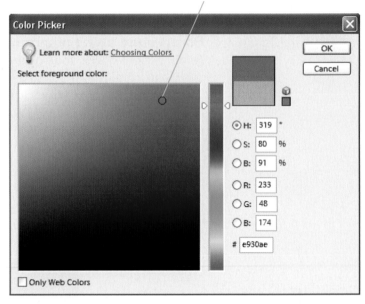

If you are going to be using images on the Web, check on the Only Web Colors box. This will display a different range of colors, which are known as Web-safe colors. This means that they will appear the same on any type of Web browser.

3 Click OK

Color Swatches palette

The Color Swatches palette can be used to access different color palettes that can then be used to select the foreground and background colors. To do this:

When the cursor is moved over a color in the Color Swatches palette, the tooltip displays the color's hexadecimal value. This is a six character sequence which displays the color in terms of the amount of red, green and blue it contains. Hexadecimal color values are made up of three groups of two characters and they consist of numbers 0–6 and letters A–F.

1 Select Window>Color Swatches from the Menu bar

2 Click here to access the available palettes

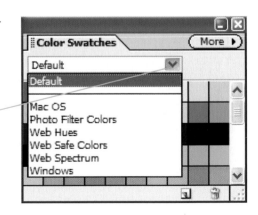

Effects and filters

One of the most exciting aspects of digital imaging is the ability to create stunning special effects. This chapter looks at some of the effects that can be used in Elements and shows you how to apply them.

Covers

Chapter Nine

Applying effects

Applying effects is one of the most satisfying parts of digital image editing: it is quick and the results can be dramatic. Effects can be applied to entire images, or to a selected area. Effects are created using the Effects palette. To apply effects:

1 Open an image (if required, a selection can be made, in which case the effect will only be applied to the selected area)

To display the items in the Effects palette as a list, click the More button and select List View.

2 Select Window>Styles and Effects from the Menu bar

3 Click here to access the available effects

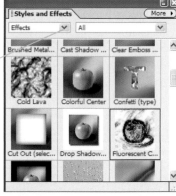

Effects can be applied to type as well as images and there are some effects specifically designed for this.

4 Double-click on an effect for it to be applied to the currently selected image or selection

Examples of effects

Blizzard

If you do not like a particular effect, click on the Step Backward button on the Shortcuts bar after it has been applied.

Colorful Center

Lizard skin

Do not get too carried away with effects and start adding them on top of each other.

Neon nights

Applying filters

Filters can be used to create similar results to effects; however, for most filters there is an additional dialog so you can edit their attributes. Filters can be used on entire images or selected areas.

To use filters:

1 Open an image or select part of an image

The available filters can also be accessed from the Filter menu on the Menu bar.

2 Click here in the Styles and Effects palette to access the available filters

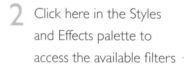

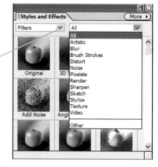

Additional filters can also be accessed from the dialog boxes of individual filters.

3 Double-click on a filter to access its related dialog box

4 Make the required selections for the filter and click OK

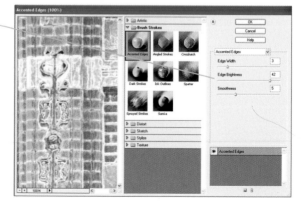

Examples of filters

Bas Relief
Select options for the effect here and click OK.

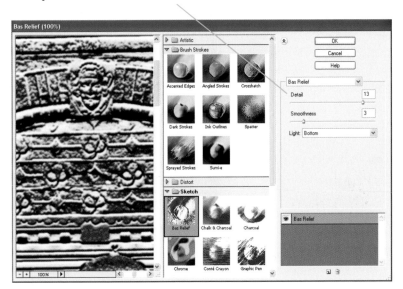

In general, it is not a good idea to add a filter to an image that has already had one applied to it. This just serves to lessen the impact of both of the filters used.

Neon Glow
Select options for the effect here and click OK.

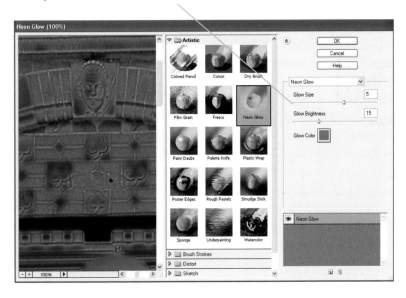

Mosaic Tiles

Select options for the effect here and click OK.

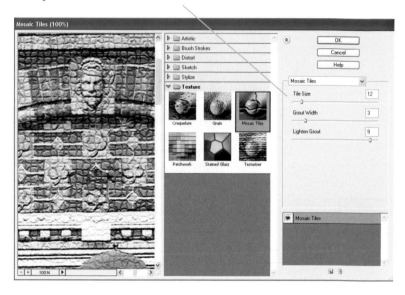

Lens Flare

Some filters have simpler dialog boxes, where there are only options for that specific filter, rather than a dialog box that allows you to select other filters too.

The Lens Flare filter creates effects similar to those that occur through a camera lens when light shines through the lens at a particular angle.

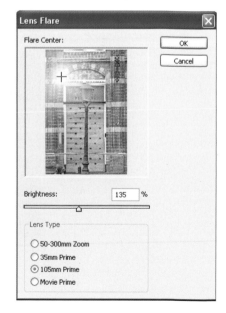

Liquify filter

The Liquify filter is an option that can be accessed by selecting Filter>Distort>Liquify from the Menu bar or from the Liquify option on the Filters palette. It has its own window from which various options can be selected for different liquify effects.

Creating a reflection

To create a reflection of an image in the liquify filter

If you want to reflect an area from below the Reflection tool, drag it from left to right.

1 Select the reflection tool

2 Drag the reflection tool from right to left under the area of the image that you want to reflect

3 Select the Warp tool

4 Drag the Warp tool diagonally across the reflected part of the image to give it a more rippled effect

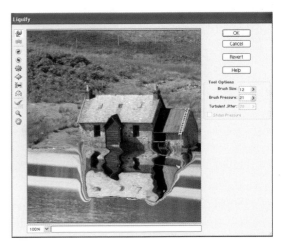

Warping, puckering and bloating

These tools, which are available within the Liquify filter, can be used for, among other things, changing facial expressions:

1 Original image

2 Select the Warp tool to achieve distortion

The tools in the Liquify filter are (from top to bottom): Warp, Turbulence, Twirl Clockwise, Twirl Counter Clockwise, Pucker, Bloat, Shift Pixels, Reflection, Reconstruct, Zoom and Hand.

3 Select the Pucker tool and drag it on the image to decrease the size of areas within it

4 Select the Bloat tool and drag it on the image to increase the size of areas within it

Sharing and creating

Sharing images with other people and creating artistic projects are now important aspects of digital photography. This chapter shows a variety of ways in which images can be shared and also details several projects that can be undertaken to produce eye-catching photographic creations. It also looks at some of the issues connected with using images on the Web.

Covers

Saving images for the Web

The most crucial issue for images that are going to be used on the Web is file size. This must be small enough so that the images can be downloaded quickly on a Web page, otherwise the user will become impatient and move on to another site. To assist in this, Elements has a function for saving images in different formats and also altering the quality settings for each format. This enables you to balance the image quality and file size so that you have the optimum image for use on the Web. To do this:

Try to keep images that are going to be used on the Web well under 100K in file size. If possible, a file size in the region of 30–50K is desirable.

1 Open an image and select File>Save for Web from the Menu bar

2 The original image is shown on the left of the Save for Web window

3 Select options for optimizing the image for the Web here

Preparing images for the Web is also known as optimizing them.

4 The preview of the optimized image is shown here, once the settings have been applied. The new file size and download time at a specified speed are shown below the image

5 Click here to select a file format

6 Click here to select a compression setting

7 Click here to select a quality setting

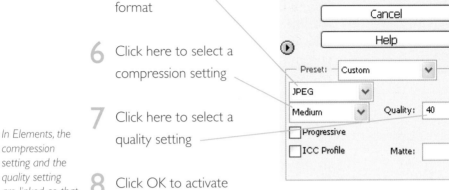

> **BEWARE**
>
> *In Elements, the compression setting and the quality setting are linked, so that when one is altered the other is changed automatically. A low compression setting equates to a low quality value, and so on.*

8 Click OK to activate the Save Optimized As window. By default, the file is saved with the same name as the original. To avoid overwriting the original, give the file a new name and click Save

> **DON'T FORGET**
>
> *Even low-quality images can look good on Web pages, as computer monitors are more forgiving in their image output than hard copy printing is.*

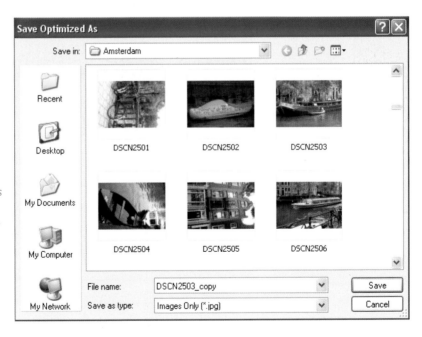

Emailing images

One of the most common ways of transferring images electronically is by email. However, the same rules apply here as with images on the Web – the file size should be as small as possible. A good way to alienate friends and work colleagues is to send them large attachments as part of an email. It is not uncommon for people to send images over 1Mb in size, which can take several minutes to download. Elements takes this into account when attaching images to emails, but it is also worth optimizing them yourself before you attach them to an email. Rather than having to open your email program separately, Elements has a function for attaching images directly to an email and also creating artistic effects with stationery and templates. To do this:

1 Open an image in the Editor or select it in the Photo Browser

2 Click on this icon in the Editor, or select Share>Email from the Shortcuts bar in the Photo Browser

Images that are attached to emails are automatically compressed by Elements to make it quicker to send them over the Internet.

3 Click here and select Photo Mail (HTML) to use a template

4 Click here to select an email recipient

5 Click here to add photos

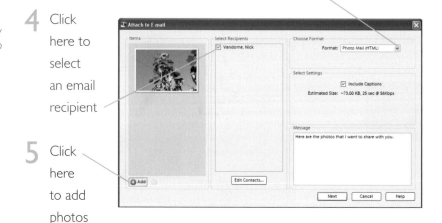

6 Click here to select a stationery style and click Next Step

As well as email addresses, images can also be sent to mobile phones or shared online. However, you have to have access to the appropriate services for this. Check with your Internet Service Provider for details.

7 Click here to select a background and a layout style. Click Next

8 The stationery style and image will be attached to an email with a message pre-inserted in the Subject box. This can be edited if required

Creating a slide show

As more and more people are using digital images, so it is becoming more common for them to want to share them in ever-increasingly artistic ways. Elements addresses this issue with a section dedicated entirely to ways of sharing images creatively. This can be accessed from either the Editor or the Organizer by clicking on the Create icon:

The first project in the Create section is for creating slide shows, which can then be saved or copied to disc to share with other people. To do this:

Click here to start creating a slide show

If an image is already selected in the Photo Browser it will be the first one that is visible in the slide show window.

Select settings for the slide show and click OK

Video can be included in slide shows in .avi, .mpeg or .wmv file formats.

3 Click here to add photos, video or audio to the slide show

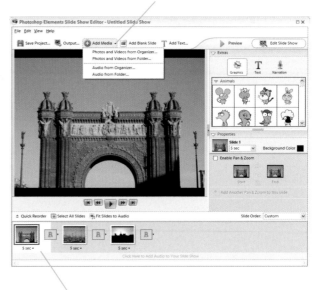

Video and audio can be selected either from the default collection in the Organizer or from your own collection elsewhere on your hard drive.

4 Items in the slide show are displayed here on the timeline

The content in a slide show can be previewed in the editing window by using the playback controls under the main content area.

5 Click and drag a cartoon figure to add it to an element within the slide show

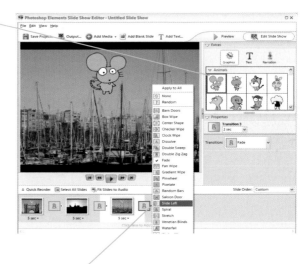

6 Click here to edit the transitions between elements of the slide show

7 Click here to select
an output option

8 Select an output
option for the
slide show and
click OK

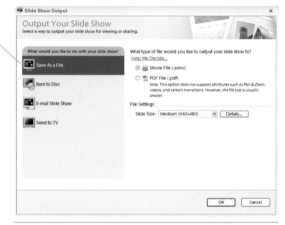

or

*A completed
slide show can
be burned to CD
from the options
accessed from
the Output button. Also, if the
slide show has been saved as
a creation you can select the
creation thumbnail in the Photo
Browser and select Edit>Burn a
Video CD from the Menu bar.*

9 Click here to save
the current project

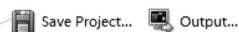 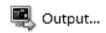

10 Give your slide show a name and click Save

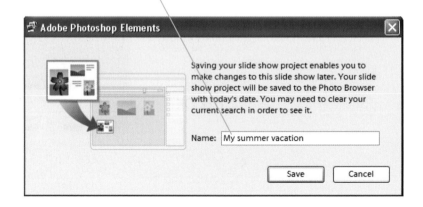

Viewing creations

Once an item has been made in the Create section it is added to the Photo Browser. It can then be viewed as follows:

1 Each creation is added to the Photo Browser and the fact that it is a creation is denoted by this icon

2 Double-click on the thumbnail to open the creation

Alternatively

1 Select File>Open Creation in the Organizer

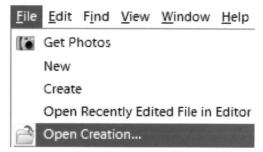

2 Select the Creation to be opened and click OK

Creating a VCD

If you want to view your slide shows on television via a DVD player, or share them with other people in this format, this can be done by creating a VCD. This is similar to a DVD except that it is created on a CD. This enables it to be played back on a DVD player, without the need to burn it onto a DVD disc with a DVD writer. To create a VCD:

1 Click here on the Creation menu and click OK

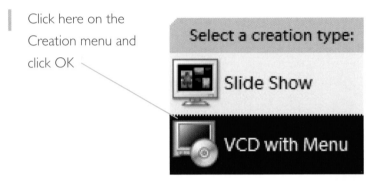

The VCD (VideoCD) format enables CDs to be used in DVD players. The quality is not as good as that of a DVD and a CD can only hold approximately 700 Mb of data, as opposed to 4 Gb on a DVD. Nevertheless, they are a very good option for viewing photos and slide shows.

2 Click here to add slide shows. Several slide shows can be added to a single VCD

The VCD Creation project offers more flexibility than simply burning the slide show to a CD, as it also creates a menu for the start of the CD. This uses the first thumbnail image from each slide show.

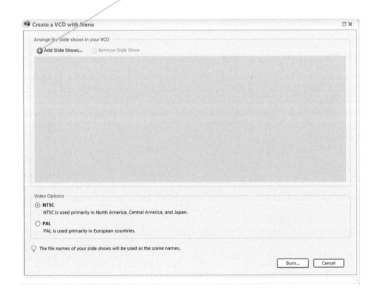

3 Check the boxes next to the slide shows that you want to add to the VCD

4 Click OK

5 The slide shows to be used on the VCD are displayed here

The video options are selected according to where you will be viewing the VCD: NTSC format is used mainly in North America, Central America and Japan while the PAL format is used mainly in Europe.

6 Select a video format here

7 Click Burn

Creating album pages

The Album Pages option can be used to create a book of photos using preset designs. The book can then be printed out in its entirety. To do this:

1 Click here on the Creation menu and click OK

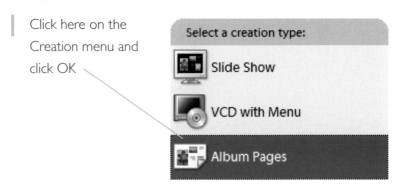

2 Click here to select a style for the album pages

3 Click Next Step

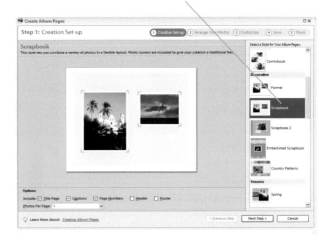

4 Click here to add photos to the album pages

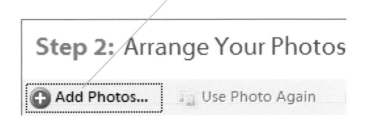

5 Check the boxes next to the photos you want to use

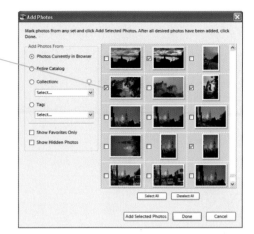

6 Click Done

7 Check that you have the right photos and click Next Step

When you are adding captions to the images in the album pages, a dialog box will appear with various text formatting options, which are applied in the album.

8 Double-click here and add a caption for each image. Click Next Step

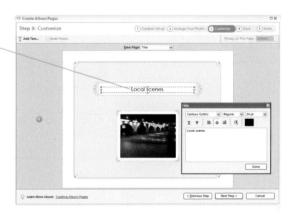

9 Enter a name for the album pages here

Once album pages have been created they can be saved as a PDF file, printed, emailed to people or shared online (depending on available services). This enables you to share your album pages with others; otherwise, you could only share them with other people who are using Elements.

10 Click here to select an option for sharing the album pages

11 Click Save to save the album pages to the Photo Browser

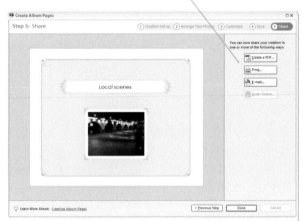

When selecting to print album pages, there are no additional print options as the album pages are viewed as a self-contained project.

12 To print the album pages, select the album's thumbnail in the Photo Browser and select File>Print from the Menu bar. The whole album will be printed

Creating cards and postcards

Cards and postcards can be created using your own images, and the process is similar for both:

1 Select one of the cards options on the Creation menu and click OK

2 Select a template style and click Next Step

3 Click here to select your own image and click Next Step

4 Double-click to add a caption and click Next Step

5 Give the card a title and click Save

You can now save your creation to edit it later.

4-Fold Greeting Card Name:

Greetings from Edinburgh

Creating a calendar

An excellent way to use your own images creatively, either for yourself or as a gift for others, is to incorporate them into a calendar. To do this:

1 Click here on the Creation menu and click OK

2 Click here to select a style for the calendar

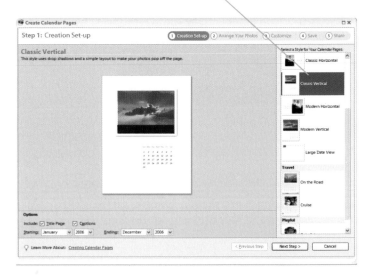

3 Select the options for the date format of the calendar and click Next Step

4 Click here to add photos for the calendar

Thirteen photos should be added for an annual calendar, i.e. one for each month of the year and one for the cover.

5 Click Next Step

6 Double-click here to add text for the cover page of the calendar

7 Click Next Step

Double-Click to Insert Title

8 Enter a title for the calendar creation. Click Save and then click Done

You can now save your creation to edit it later.

Calendar Pages Name:

Barcelona vacation

☐ Use Title for Name

An entire calendar can be printed by selecting it in the Photo Browser and selecting Edit>Print from the Menu bar. If there are any problems with the format of the calendar, e.g. there are missing images, you will be alerted to this before the printing starts.

9 Once the calendar has been created it can be accessed for viewing in the same way as other creations, i.e. by double-clicking on its creation icon in the Photo Browser. Click here to preview each month of the calendar. Once the calendar is completed it can be printed, sent to someone via email or converted into a PDF file

View Page: April 2006 ▼

April   2006

Sun Mon Tue Wed Thu Fri Sat

                                    1
2   3   4   5   6   7   8
9   10   11   12   13   14   15
16 17   18   19   20   21   22
23 24   25   26   27   28   29
30

Creating an HTML photo gallery

Another way of sharing images is to place them on your own personal Web page. If this is done manually, it requires some knowledge of HTML (Hypertext Markup Language), which is the code used to create most Web pages. However, in the Creation section it is possible to create photo galleries for the Web with no knowledge of HTML, as Elements takes care of all of that behind the scenes. To do this:

To find out more about HTML see "HTML in easy steps".

1 Click here on the Creation menu and click OK

2 Click here to select a style for the HTML photo gallery

For more information about general Web page creation see "Creating Web Pages in easy steps".

3 Click here to add photos for the HTML photo gallery

If you want to add images from different locations, select the initial images and click the Add Selected Photos button. Then move to another location and repeat the process. When all of the required photos have been obtained, click OK.

4 To add photos, select a location and check the boxes next to the images to be included. Click Done

The text and formatting options determine the appearance of the HTML photo gallery and which items appear in the published gallery, such as title and email address.

5 The images to be included are displayed here

6 Click here to select options for adding text and for formatting the final HTML gallery

You have to select a file location for the HTML photo gallery and give it a specific name in the Site Folder box. When the HTML photo gallery is saved, this folder is created and all of the HTML photo gallery files are saved within it.

7 Click Save

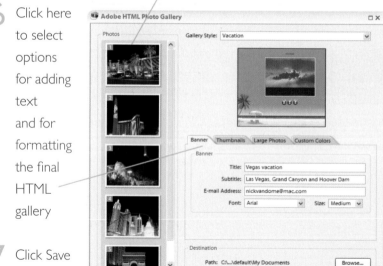

8 The HTML photo gallery is created automatically by Elements. All of the HTML is created in the background

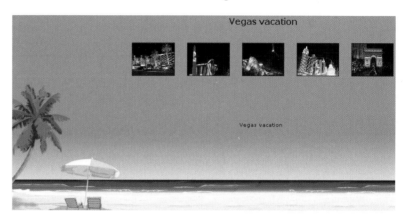

Once the HTML photo gallery has been completed it can be viewed on the Web. This can be done by acquiring your own domain name and using a Web hosting service. Alternatively, you could use a free Web hosting service such as those offered by Yahoo Geocities and AOL.

9 Navigate to the folder that you have specified for the HTML photo gallery. Double-click on the Index file to view the HTML photo gallery

When loading the HTML photo gallery onto the Web, upload the whole folder in which the files are located. This is necessary because several additional files will have been created to ensure the correct operation of the HTML photo gallery.

10 The HTML photo gallery will be displayed in your default Web browser. Click on these buttons to navigate through the gallery

Backing up

If you have a large number of photos stored digitally on your computer, the biggest fear is that you will lose them, either through a technical malfunction, such as a major hard disk crash, or through a physical event such as a fire. Because of this, it is essential that you back up your image files at regular intervals. This can be done through Elements by copying selected files, or entire catalogs, to CD. To do this:

The Copy/Move option can be used to move files off your hard drive and copy them onto a CD for archiving purposes. If you do this, make sure you do not still need to use the files in the near future.

1   In Photo Browser select File>Backup from the Menu bar

2   Click here to select the whole catalog in the Photo Browser to be backed up and click Next

3   Elements will check for any files that have been moved since they were imported. Click Reconnect to have them included in the backup

The initial backup of a whole catalog will take longer than subsequent incremental backups.

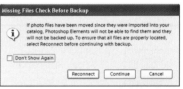

4   Click here for the initial, full, backup of your files. Click Next

Depending on the size of your image catalog you may require more than one CD with which to back it up. If this is the case a warning box will inform you of how many discs are required.

5   Put a CD in your CD burner; select the required drive on your computer. Click Done to proceed with the backup and have your files burned onto CD

Printing images

Printing digital images is one of their most common uses and the quality is now comparable with that of traditional film photographs. This chapter looks at general printing issues, how to size images for printing and how to select the best layout format for your printed output.

Covers

Chapter Eleven

Printing issues

Three of the top inkjet printer manufacturers are Epson, Canon and Hewlett Packard. Their websites can be found at (respectively):

- www.epson.com
- www.canon.com
- www.hp.com

Printers

One of the biggest advances in the digital imaging process in recent years has been in the quality of the images when they are printed. Printers can now produce images that are of virtually the same quality as images processed from traditional film cameras. There are three main types of printer that can be used to print digital images:

- Inkjet printers. These are the cheapest and the most common. In addition, they also produce excellent results. They work by placing tiny dots of color on the paper to make up the image

- Laser printers. Color laser printers are expensive and they are generally only a viable option in the workplace

- Dye-sublimation and thermal wax printers. Unlike inkjet printers, these printers place a continuous coating of ink on the paper rather than a series of dots. They produce excellent results but are more expensive than inkjet printers and do not have the same versatility in terms of paper size

The CMYK color model is used to create printed images since printers cannot produce the exact same colors as the eye sees, which are represented by the RGB (Red, Green, Blue) color model. In CMYK Black is denoted by K rather than B so as not to confuse it with Blue.

Ink

When looking at printers, the question of ink is also an important one. Inkjet printers use a minimum of four color cartridges (Cyan, Magenta, Yellow and Black, which produce the CMYK color model). Some printers have an extra two, or even four, cartridges, which are usually variations of Cyan and Magenta, and produce more subtle skin tones. When looking at printers, check the cost of replacement cartridges as this could be an important factor in the overall running costs of the printer.

Paper

There is a huge variety of paper available for printing digital images. If you want to get the very best results:

Some companies sell non-branded ink cartridges. While these are cheaper than the branded versions, the quality is not always as high.

- Buy the same make of paper as your printer. This may be more expensive than other brands but it will be the most compatible with your printer and its printing technology

- Use the heaviest photo quality paper available

Calibrating your monitor

One of the issues with digital images is achieving consistency between different computer monitors and also output devices, such as printers. Inconsistency means that the colors can appear different if they are viewed on several monitors and also that the colors in the printed image may not match those viewed on screen. One way to try to achieve as much consistency as possible is to calibrate your monitor before you start working with digital images. This is particularly important if you are going to be sharing images with other people for editing purposes, in which case they should calibrate their monitors too. This will ensure that images look as similar as possible on different machines and so editing can be applied consistently.

To calibrate your monitor:

1. Make sure your monitor and computer have been turned on for at least 30 minutes

2. Set the monitor display to a minimum of 16-bit color (or thousands of colors) and set the background color as neutral

To access the Display Properties click the Start button and select Control Panel>Appearance and Themes> Display; then click on the Settings tab.

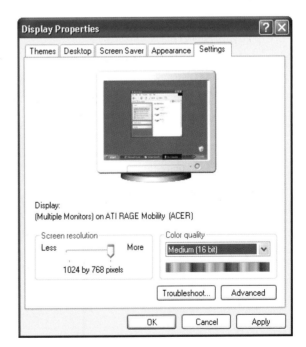

3 Click the Start button and select Control Panel

4 Select Appearances and Themes and double-click the Adobe
Gamma button

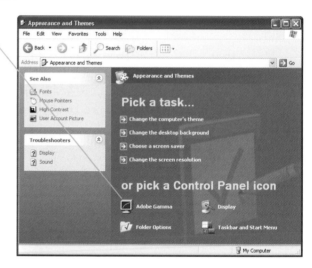

5 Check on the Step by Step (Wizard) box and click Next to follow
the wizard's steps

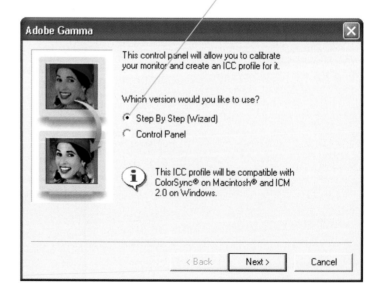

6 Click Finish at the end of the wizard

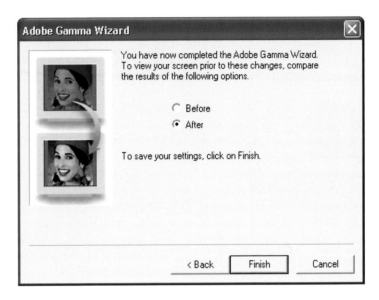

7 Save the color profile that has been created

By default, new color profiles are stored in the **color** *folder on your computer.*

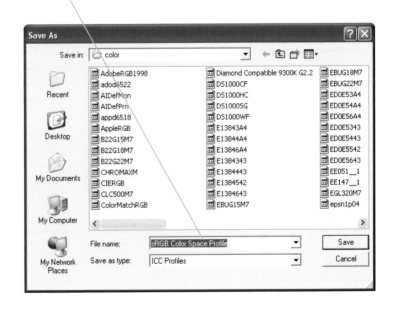

Print size

Before you start printing images in Elements it is important to ensure that they are going to be produced at the required size. Since the pixels within an image are not a set size, the printed dimensions of an image can be altered according to your needs. This is done by specifying how many pixels are used within each inch of the image. The more pixels per inch (ppi) then the higher the quality of the printed image, but the smaller in size it will be.

The higher the resolution in the Document Size section of the dialog, the greater the quality but the smaller the size of the printed image.

To set the print size of an image:

1 Open an image and select Image>Resize>Image Size from the Menu bar

2 Uncheck the Resample Image box. This will ensure that the physical image size, i.e. the number of pixels in the image, remains unchanged when the resolution is changed

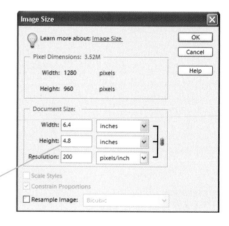

The output size for a printed image can be worked out by dividing the pixel dimensions (the width and height) by the resolution. So if the width is 1280, the height 960 and the resolution 300, the printed image will be roughly 4 inches by 3 inches.

3 The current resolution and document size (print size) are displayed here

4 Enter a new figure in the Resolution box (here the resolution has been increased from 200 to 300). This affects the Document size, i.e. the size at which the image prints

An image of 1280 × 960 pixels, set to print at 150 pixels per inch (not actual size)

To achieve the best results, print images at a resolution of 200 ppi or above and set your printer to its highest dots per inch (dpi) setting. On current inkjet printers this is in the range of up to 5760 dpi.

Dots per inch (dpi) and pixels per inch (ppi) are not the same. The term "dots per inch" refers to the colored dots produced by the printer and "pixels per inch" refers to the number of colored dots within an inch of the image itself.

An image of 1280 × 960 pixels, set to print at 300 pixels per inch (not actual size)

As long as the Resample box is unchecked, changing the output resolution has no effect on the actual number of pixels in an image.

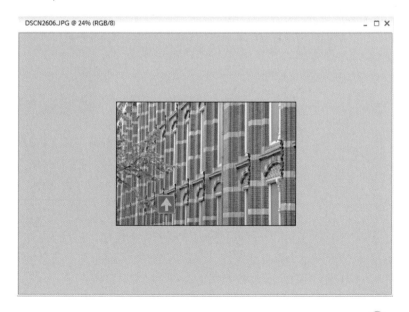

Print Preview

The Print Preview function can be used to view how an image will look when it is printed. This can be a useful option for ensuring you do not waste too much paper when printing images.

To use Print Preview:

1 Select File>Print from the Menu bar

To preview the print size of an image without accessing Print Preview, select the Zoom tool from the Toolbox and click the Print Size button in the Options bar.

2 Check the Center Image box to center the image on the page when it is printed

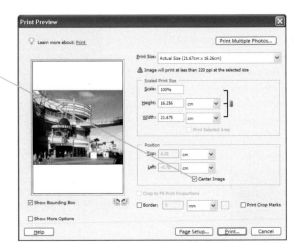

3 Uncheck the Center Image box and drag the image elsewhere. Or specify a location from the top left of the paper

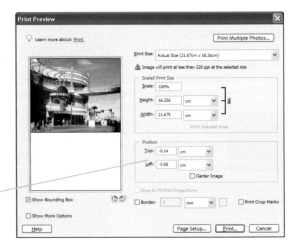

Printing multiple photos

When printing images it is useful to be able to print multiple copies at the same time and also print more than one image at a time. This can be achieved with the Print Multiple Photos command. To do this:

1 Open one or more images in the Editor

DSCN0417.jpg   dp_examples.jpg

The Print Multiple Photos option gives more flexibility than just changing the number of prints in the normal Print dialog box.

2 Select File>Print Multiple Photos from the Menu bar

3 Click here to select a print size for the images

4 Click here to add more images for printing

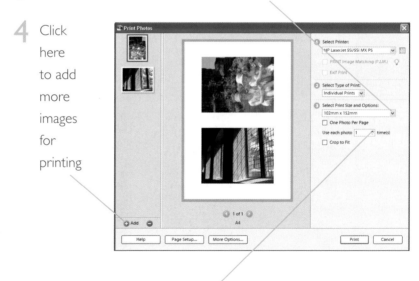

5 Click here to specify the number of printed copies required for each image. Click Print

Print Layouts

Rather than just offering the sole function of printing a single image on a sheet of paper, Elements has two options that can be used when printing images, which can help reduce the number of sheets of paper used.

Contact Sheets

This can be used to create and print thumbnail versions of a large number of images. To do this:

1 Access the Photo Browser and select the required images

2 Select File>Print from the Menu bar

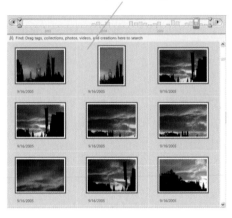

3 Click here and select Contact Sheet

4 Click Print. The selected images will be printed as thumbnails on a single sheet, or sheets

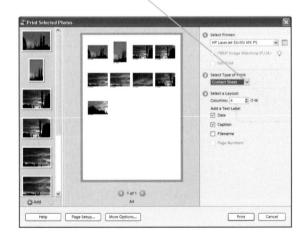

Picture Package

This can be used to print out copies of different images on a single piece of paper. To do this:

1 Access the Photo Browser and select the required images

When buying a printer, choose one that has borderless printing. This means that it can print to the very edge of the page. This is particularly useful for items such as files produced as a Picture Package.

2 Select File>Print, or click on this icon and select Print

3 Click here to select the Picture Package print option

4 Click here to select the layout for the Picture Package

The Picture Package function is a useful one for printing images in a combination of sizes, such as for family portraits.

5 Click Print

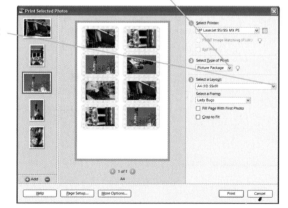

Creating PDF files

PDF (Portable Document Format) is a file format that is used to maintain the original formatting and style of a document so that it can be viewed on a variety of different devices and types of computers. In general, it is usually used for documents that contain text and images such as information pamphlets, magazine features and chapters from books. However, image files such as JPEGs can also be converted into PDF and this can be done within Elements without the need for any other special software. To do this:

1 Open a file and select File>Save As from the Menu bar

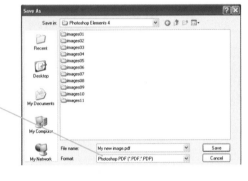

PDF files are an excellent way to share files so that other people can print them. All that is required is a copy of Adobe Acrobat Reader, which is bundled with most software packages on computers, or can be downloaded from the Adobe website at www.adobe.com

2 Select a destination folder and make sure the format is set to Photoshop PDF. Then click Save

3 The PDF file is created and can be opened in Adobe Acrobat or Elements

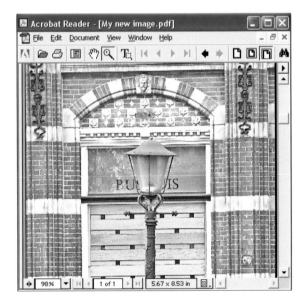

Index